Copyright Page

Lawyer's SEO Playbook: Drive Organic Traffic and Grow Your Firm
Copyright © 2024 by Adam Jabbar

All rights reserved. No part of this book may be reproduced, distributed, or transmitted in any form or by any means, including photocopying, recording, or other electronic or mechanical methods, without the prior written permission of the publisher, except in the case of brief quotations embodied in critical reviews and certain other non-commercial uses permitted by copyright law. For permission requests, contact the publisher at the address below.

Publisher:
Adam Jabbar

This book is a work of non-fiction. While every effort has been made to ensure accuracy, the author and publisher assume no responsibility for errors, omissions, or for outcomes resulting from the use of the information contained herein.

First Edition: 2024

ABOUT THE AUTHOR

Adam Jabbar is a technology lawyer and a writer with a unique blend of legal and business expertise. He holds a Bachelor of Law (LLB) from the University of London and a Bachelor of Business Administration (BBA) from Heriot-Watt University. This diverse educational background gave Adam the insight and inspiration to develop SEO content tailored specifically for law firms, blending his passion for law and digital marketing.

Adam is also the author of the Amazon bestseller "ChatGPT for Lawyers: 101 Practical Prompts," a powerful tool for attorneys looking to streamline their workflows using AI technology.

He is also a top-rated seller on Fiverr, where he has provided SEO and content solutions for over 1,000 personal injury and estate planning blogs, helping law firms enhance their online presence and attract more clients through effective, SEO-friendly content strategies.

With his practical and results-driven approach, Adam focuses on making complex SEO concepts accessible and useful for legal professionals. His work bridges the gap between legal expertise and digital marketing, empowering law firms to thrive in the digital age.

INTRODUCTION: WHY SEO MATTERS FOR LAWYERS

Welcome to the "Lawyer's SEO Playbook," where we break down the strategies and tactics that will help your law firm not just survive, but thrive in the digital age. This isn't another generic marketing book filled with vague ideas or surface-level advice. Instead, it's designed to guide you through the often-misunderstood world of Search Engine Optimization (SEO) specifically tailored for law firms. By the time you've finished this book, you'll have a clear, actionable roadmap to driving organic traffic to your website and turning that traffic into high-value clients.

The Digital Shift: Understanding the Modern Client Journey

In today's world, nearly everyone turns to Google or another search engine when they need legal services. Think about it—when was the last time you grabbed a phone book to find a professional service? Probably years ago. Your potential clients are no different.

Whether they need help with family law, personal injury claims, business litigation, or criminal defense, the first step most clients take is to open up a search engine and type in what they need. They don't just search for "lawyer," though—they're more specific. They'll type "personal injury lawyer near me" or "divorce attorney in [city name]." And if your law firm's website isn't appearing on the first page of results, those potential clients are likely clicking on your competitor's site instead.

This is why SEO matters more than ever for law firms. SEO isn't just about ranking higher in search engines—it's about putting your firm in front of the clients who are actively looking for your services. It's about getting discovered at the exact moment someone needs legal help. The firms that can be found quickly and easily are the ones that will win clients consistently.

The Power of Organic Traffic

If you've ever dabbled in digital marketing before, you've probably come across the term "organic traffic." Simply put, organic traffic refers to visitors who come to your website through unpaid search results. This is different from paid ads, where you spend money to appear at the top of Google or social media platforms. Organic traffic, on the other hand, is driven by SEO—optimizing your website so it naturally ranks higher in search engines without having to pay for every click.

Why is organic traffic so valuable? For one, it's sustainable. While paid ads stop generating leads the moment you stop paying for them, SEO continues to work for you 24/7, even while you sleep. It's a long-term investment that, once built, keeps bringing in clients without draining your marketing budget.

But here's the thing: Not all traffic is created equal. You don't just want random visitors to your website—you want the right visitors. People who are genuinely searching for legal services in your area and are ready to take action. That's where SEO, when done correctly, comes in. It helps ensure that the people landing on your website are more likely to be those looking for exactly what you offer.

What to Expect From This Playbook

Unlike many other SEO guides out there, this book is designed specifically for lawyers and law firms. I won't waste your time with abstract marketing jargon or impractical strategies. Instead, I'll show you exactly what works for law firms of all sizes, based on real-world experience and proven techniques.

Here's what you can expect to learn:

- The Basics: If you're new to SEO, don't worry—we'll start by covering the fundamentals in simple terms. You'll learn exactly what SEO is, how it works, and why it's essential for your firm.
- Building a Strong Foundation: We'll cover the key steps to make your law firm's website Google-friendly, from technical aspects like site speed and mobile optimization to on-page SEO strategies like using the right keywords and structuring your content.
- Content is King: Learn how to create content that not only ranks well but also resonates with potential clients. We'll cover blog posts, service pages, and how to write in a way that converts visitors into paying clients.
- Local SEO: For most law firms, local clients are the lifeblood of their business. I'll show you how to optimize for local searches so that you show up when someone in your area is looking for a lawyer.
- Advanced Strategies: Once you've mastered the basics, we'll dive into more advanced tactics like link building, voice search optimization, and using video to boost your rankings.

But this book isn't just about driving traffic. It's about driving the right traffic. You'll learn how to turn visitors into clients, how to track your results, and how to continuously improve your SEO efforts over time. Because SEO isn't a one-time job—it's a long-term strategy that, when done right, will fuel your firm's growth for years to come.

This Isn't Just Theory—It's Actionable

Many SEO books are filled with vague advice, leaving you wondering, "What do I actually do with this information?" This playbook is different. Each chapter will include actionable steps you can take right away. By the end of this book, you'll not only understand how SEO works but also have a clear plan of how to apply it to your law firm.

Whether you're a solo practitioner or managing a large firm, the SEO strategies in this book will help you stand out in a crowded digital landscape and consistently bring in new clients.

> *Let's get started. Your next client is searching for legal help right now. The question is—will they find you?*

CHAPTER 1: SEO BASICS FOR LAWYERS

Let's get real for a second. SEO (Search Engine Optimization) might seem like some mystical marketing buzzword, but at its core, it's just about one simple thing: making sure people can find you online when they're looking for legal help. Imagine you've got a billboard for your law firm, but it's tucked away in a dark alley where nobody goes. SEO is like taking that billboard and planting it on the busiest street in town. The goal? Get your law firm noticed by the right people at the right time.

In this chapter, we'll break down SEO in plain English, with examples to show you how it all works. No jargon. No confusing tech speak. Just straightforward steps to help you understand why SEO is crucial and how it can bring more clients through your door.

What is SEO, and Why Should You Care?

Let's start with a question: **What's the first thing someone does when they need a lawyer?** They pull out their phone or sit at their computer and head straight to Google. They don't call their cousin or flip through a phone book (if those even exist anymore). If you're not showing up in those search results, someone else is getting that call.

Here's the deal: **SEO (Search Engine Optimization)** is the process of making your website more visible in search engines like Google. When someone types in "divorce lawyer near me" or "personal injury attorney in [city]," you want your law firm to show up on that first page of results. The higher you rank, the more likely you are to get the click, the call, and the client.

Why is this so important? Well, **75% of people never scroll past the first page of Google results**. If your law firm's website isn't ranking high enough, potential clients are skipping right over you and going to your competitors.

Example Time:

Imagine you're a personal injury lawyer in Miami. A potential client types "best personal injury lawyer Miami" into Google. If your website is well-optimized, it could show up near the top of the results. If not, that client might end up calling another lawyer, simply because they were easier to find.

Why SEO is Critical for Law Firms

You're a lawyer, not a marketer. So why should you care about SEO? Because your next client is out there searching for you right now. And if you're not easily found, you're missing out.

Here's why SEO is especially important for law firms:

- **Legal services are hyper-local**: Most people are looking for a lawyer in their city, or even their specific neighborhood. SEO helps you rank well in local searches like "estate planning attorney [your city]."

- **Clients start their journey online**: More than **95% of people use search engines** to find legal services. If you're not showing up, you're not part of their decision-making process.

- **SEO builds trust**: When potential clients see your firm ranking high in search results, they automatically assume you're credible. Why? Because they trust Google to show them the best results.

Key SEO Terms You Need to Know (With Examples!)

I promised to keep this simple, and I will. But there are a few key SEO terms you need to understand before we go deeper. Let's break these down with some easy-to-understand examples.

1. **Keywords**:
   - **What are they?** Keywords are the words or phrases that people type into Google when they're searching for something.
   - **Example**: If someone types "family lawyer in New York," that entire phrase is a **keyword**. It's what your potential client is using to find legal help, so you need to make sure your website uses these kinds of phrases.

2. **SERP (Search Engine Results Page)**:
   - **What is it?** It's the page Google shows after someone enters a search.
   - **Example**: If you Google "criminal defense attorney," the list of results you see is called the **SERP**. Your goal is to get your law firm's website on that first page of the SERP.

3. **Organic Traffic**:
   - **What is it?** Visitors who come to your website through unpaid search results.
   - **Example**: If someone finds your law firm's website after searching "bankruptcy lawyer near me" and clicks on your site (without you paying for an ad), that's **organic traffic**.

4. **Backlinks**:
   - **What are they?** These are links from other websites to your website. They're like votes of confidence from other sites, telling Google your site is trustworthy.
   - **Example**: If a legal blog writes an article about "Top 10 Divorce Lawyers in [Your City]" and includes a link to your website, that's a **backlink**. The more quality backlinks you have,

the better your chances of ranking higher.

5. **On-Page SEO**:
   - **What is it?** This is the practice of optimizing individual web pages to help them rank higher. It includes things like the content you write, your headlines, and even how fast your site loads.
   - **Example**: Let's say you write a blog post titled "What to Do After a Car Accident in [Your City]." If you include the right keywords (like "car accident lawyer" and "personal injury attorney") and structure the page well, you've nailed **on-page SEO**.

6. **Off-Page SEO**:
   - **What is it?** It refers to actions taken outside your own website to boost its ranking—like getting those backlinks or managing your online reputation.
   - **Example**: If you write guest articles for other legal websites, those links back to your own site help your **off-page SEO**.

7. **Domain Authority**:
   - **What is it?** This is a score that predicts how well your website will rank on search engines.
   - **Example**: A large law firm with lots of high-quality content and backlinks will have a higher **domain authority** than a brand-new website with no content. The higher your domain authority, the better your chances of showing up high in search results.

8. **Meta Tags**:
   - **What are they?** These are snippets of code that tell search engines what your page is about.

- **Example**: When you see a search result that looks like this:

How Clients Actually Search for Legal Services

Let's take a step back and think about how your clients actually search for legal help. They're not typing in fancy legal jargon like "litigation attorney" or "tort law specialist." They're typing in questions or simple phrases that relate to their situation.

- **Example 1**: Someone who's been in a car accident isn't searching for "negligence attorney"; they're typing "what to do after a car accident" or "car accident lawyer near me."
- **Example 2**: A couple considering divorce might search for "how to file for divorce in [city]" instead of "family law attorney."

You need to understand your clients' mindset. Think about their problems, their fears, and the questions they're asking Google. **The better you can answer those questions on your website, the more likely you are to attract them as clients.**

Avoiding Common SEO Myths

SEO can feel overwhelming at first, and you'll probably hear a lot of conflicting advice. Let's clear up some common SEO myths right now.

1. **Myth: SEO is all about cramming your site with keywords.**
    - **Truth**: While keywords are important, **Google cares about quality**. You can't just stuff your site with "personal injury lawyer" 100 times and expect to rank. It's about providing helpful, well-structured content that answers the questions potential clients are asking.
2. **Myth: You can get to the top of Google overnight.**
    - **Truth**: SEO takes time. If someone promises

you instant results, be skeptical. It's a long-term game, but the results are worth it.

3. **Myth: SEO is too complicated for lawyers.**
   - **Truth**: Yes, there's some technical stuff involved, but the basics are simple. If you can understand the legal process, you can grasp SEO. This book will walk you through it all in plain English, so you'll never feel lost.

4. **Myth: Once you rank well, your job is done.**
   - **Truth**: SEO is ongoing. You need to keep updating your site, adding fresh content, and staying on top of changes to Google's algorithm. But don't worry—we'll cover how to maintain your rankings in future chapters.

Final Thoughts on SEO Basics

SEO isn't magic. It's a process that, when done right, can transform your law firm's online presence. The key takeaway from this chapter is that **SEO is all about being found by the right people, at the right time, with the right message**. And when you do that, you're not just driving traffic—you're driving *clients*.

In the next chapter, we'll dive into **building your law firm's SEO foundation**, starting with how to optimize your website so Google loves it.

CHAPTER 2: BUILDING YOUR LAW FIRM'S SEO FOUNDATION

Now that you've got a handle on the basics of SEO, it's time to build a strong foundation. Think of SEO like constructing a house. Before you can paint the walls or hang pictures, you need a sturdy foundation to support everything else. For SEO, that foundation is your website.

In this chapter, we're going to dive into how to optimize your law firm's website to make sure Google can easily find, understand, and rank it. We'll walk through the technical must-haves, how to structure your content, and the most important elements that form the backbone of SEO.

Optimizing Your Website for Google

When Google looks at your website, it doesn't see it like a human would. It "reads" the code behind the scenes and looks at certain key elements to decide how relevant your site is to a specific search. If your site is hard for Google to understand, it won't rank well—no matter how great your content is.

Let's go over the essential technical pieces you need to get right.

1. Fast Loading Times: Because Nobody Likes to Wait

Google has been very clear about this: **page speed matters**. If your website takes too long to load, not only will Google rank it lower, but visitors are likely to leave before your page even loads. In fact, research shows that **40% of users will abandon a site if it takes**

more than 3 seconds to load. That's a lot of potential clients lost simply because of slow loading times.

Example:

Imagine a potential client, let's call her Sarah, who's been in a car accident and needs legal advice. She finds your website in Google, clicks on it, but then waits…and waits. After 5 seconds, she gives up and clicks back to the search results to try another lawyer. Sarah is gone, and she might not come back.

Solution:

- **Use tools like Google PageSpeed Insights** or **GTMetrix** to check your website's loading speed. These tools will give you a breakdown of what's slowing your site down and offer suggestions for improvement.
- Common fixes include compressing images, reducing the number of unnecessary plugins (if you're using WordPress), and using a fast hosting provider.

2. Mobile Responsiveness: Your Website Needs to Work Everywhere

Over **60% of web searches now happen on mobile devices**. If your website doesn't work well on a smartphone or tablet, you're missing out on a huge chunk of potential traffic. Not only that, but Google prioritizes mobile-friendly websites in its rankings. If your site isn't optimized for mobile, Google will push you down the search results.

Example:

Let's say John, a potential client, searches for "criminal defense lawyer near me" on his phone while sitting in a coffee shop. He clicks on your site, but it's hard to navigate because the text is too small, and the buttons are too close together. John quickly gets frustrated and clicks back to try another firm. You've lost John, and all because your site wasn't mobile-friendly.

Solution:

- Use a **responsive design**, which automatically adjusts your website's layout to fit any screen size.
- Test your website on different devices (phones, tablets, etc.) to make sure it looks good and is easy to navigate everywhere.
- **Google's Mobile-Friendly Test** is a free tool you can use to see if your site passes the mobile optimization test.

3. Secure Your Site with HTTPS

Google cares about security—so much so that it now considers **HTTPS (HyperText Transfer Protocol Secure)** a ranking factor. If your website isn't secure, not only will Google rank it lower, but visitors might also see a warning message in their browser saying "Not Secure," which can scare them away.

Example:

You've spent time and money building a great-looking website, but when potential clients visit, they see "Not Secure" in the URL bar. They don't know what that means, but it doesn't sound good. They might wonder if their personal information is at risk and leave your site.

Solution:

- Make sure your site has an SSL certificate. This encrypts the connection between your website and your visitors, keeping their information safe.
- Most web hosting providers offer **SSL certificates** for free or for a small fee. Once it's installed, your URL will start with **https://** instead of **http://**, and that "Not Secure" message will disappear.

4. User Experience: Make It Easy for Clients to Find What They Need

User experience (UX) is all about how easy and pleasant your website is to use. A clean, easy-to-navigate website makes visitors stick around longer, which tells Google your site is useful—and that can boost your rankings.

Example:

A visitor lands on your website looking for information about your services, but the homepage is cluttered with too much text, the menus are confusing, and there's no clear call to action. Frustrated, they leave your site without exploring further. You've just lost another potential client.

Solution:

- Keep your design simple and clean.
- Use **clear headings** and **subheadings** so visitors can quickly find what they're looking for.
- Make sure your **navigation menu** is intuitive, with easy-to-find links to important pages like "Contact Us," "Services," and "About."
- Include a **clear call to action** (CTA) on every page, like "Contact us for a free consultation" or "Schedule an appointment."

On-Page SEO Essentials

Once your website's technical foundation is solid, it's time to focus on **on-page SEO**—the things you can control on your site to make it easier for Google to understand what you do and rank you accordingly. This is where keywords, meta tags, and great content come into play.

1. Title Tags and Meta Descriptions: Your Website's First Impression

Your **title tag** and **meta description** are the first things potential clients see when your website shows up in search results. Think of them like your website's elevator pitch—if they're clear and compelling, people are more likely to click.

Example:

Let's say you're a personal injury lawyer in Los Angeles. If your title tag says, "Home," or something generic like, "Welcome to Our Law Firm," it's not telling Google or potential clients much. But if your title tag is **"Top Personal Injury Lawyer in Los Angeles | Free Consultation"**, it's clear what you do, and you're more likely to get clicks.

Solution:

- **Title Tag**: Keep it under 60 characters and make sure it includes your primary keyword. For example, if you're a family law attorney, you might use, **"Family Law Attorney in [City] | Divorce and Custody Services"**.
- **Meta Description**: This is the brief snippet under the title tag that describes your page. It should be around 150-160 characters and encourage people to click. For example, **"Looking for a reliable family law attorney in [City]? We specialize in divorce, child custody, and alimony cases. Call today for a free consultation."**

2. Crafting High-Quality, Keyword-Rich Content

When someone searches for legal help, they're often looking for information, not legal jargon. That's why creating high-quality content that answers potential clients' questions is crucial. Your goal is to provide helpful, easy-to-understand content that's rich in **keywords**—the phrases people are typing into Google when they need a lawyer.

Example:

You're a personal injury lawyer, and you know that people often search for "what to do after a car accident." Writing a blog post titled **"Step-by-Step Guide: What to Do After a Car Accident in [City]"** not only helps potential clients, but also signals to Google that your site is relevant for that search term.

Solution:

- **Identify the keywords** your potential clients are

searching for (we'll dive into keyword research in the next chapter).

- Write content that directly answers those questions in a way that's easy to understand. Avoid legal jargon unless you explain it.
- Use **headings and subheadings** (like H1, H2, H3 tags) to break up your content and make it easier for visitors and search engines to read.

3. Use Internal Links to Guide Visitors Through Your Site

Internal linking is the practice of linking from one page on your website to another. This helps Google understand the structure of your site and keeps visitors engaged by guiding them to related content.

Example:

If you write a blog post about "What to Do After a Car Accident," you could link to your **personal injury services page**, a page on **common types of injuries**, or a **free consultation contact form**. This keeps visitors moving through your site and signals to Google that your content is interconnected and valuable.

Solution:

- Add internal links between relevant pages on your website.
- For example, if you mention your criminal defense services in a blog post, link directly to your **Criminal Defense Services** page.

Technical SEO for Lawyers (Made Simple)

There's no need to get overwhelmed by the term "technical SEO." It simply refers to the behind-the-scenes tweaks that help Google find, crawl, and index your website more effectively. Let's keep it simple with two of the most important factors.

1. Sitemaps and Robots.txt: Helping Google Navigate Your Site

- A **sitemap** is essentially a roadmap of all the pages on your website. It helps Google understand the structure of your site and find all your important pages.
- **Robots.txt** is a file that tells search engines which pages of your site they can or cannot crawl. For example, you might not want Google to index your "Thank You" pages after someone submits a form.

Solution:

- If you're using WordPress or another website builder, you can generate a sitemap automatically. Submit it to **Google Search Console** to ensure Google is indexing all your important pages.
- Check your **robots.txt** file to make sure you're not accidentally blocking Google from crawling important pages.

2. Fix Broken Links and Duplicate Content

- **Broken links** (links that go to pages that don't exist) hurt your site's user experience and SEO. Google sees them as a sign of poor maintenance.
- **Duplicate content** is when the same content appears on multiple pages of your site (or even on other websites). Google doesn't like this and might penalize your rankings.

Solution:

- Use tools like **Google Search Console** or **Screaming Frog** to find and fix broken links.
- Avoid repeating the same content across multiple pages. Each page should have unique, valuable content.

Final Thoughts on Building Your SEO Foundation

Now that you've built a solid foundation, your website is ready to start climbing the Google rankings. Remember, SEO is a marathon, not a sprint. By optimizing your website's speed, structure, and content, you're setting yourself up for long-term success.

In the next chapter, we'll explore the art of **keyword research**—how to find out exactly what your potential clients are searching for and how to use those keywords to drive even more traffic to your site.

CHAPTER 3: KEYWORD RESEARCH – SPEAK THE LANGUAGE OF YOUR CLIENTS

Now that your website's foundation is solid, it's time to focus on one of the most crucial aspects of SEO: **keyword research**. Think of keywords as the bridge between what people are searching for and the content you're providing. By understanding how your potential clients search for legal services, you can position your law firm in front of the right people at the right time.

But here's the thing: keyword research isn't just about picking a few random words and stuffing them into your website. It's about understanding the language your clients use, the problems they're trying to solve, and the questions they're asking. In this chapter, I'll show you how to uncover those keywords and strategically use them to drive more traffic to your website.

Understanding Legal Keywords: What Are Clients Really Searching For?

When someone needs legal help, they're not searching for fancy legal jargon like "plaintiff's attorney specializing in civil tort litigation." They're typing in simple, direct phrases that describe their problem or what they're looking for.

Here's the key: **Your potential clients aren't lawyers**. They're everyday people who don't understand legal terms and processes.

They're searching for practical solutions to their problems in language they understand.

Example Time:

- **A personal injury client** isn't searching for "negligence tort litigation." They're typing "car accident lawyer near me" or "how much can I get for a car accident claim."
- **A divorce client** won't search for "family law attorney specializing in child custody." They're more likely to type "best divorce lawyer in [city]" or "how to get custody of my kids."

By understanding how clients think and what they search for, you can create content that speaks directly to their needs. The goal is to meet potential clients where they are, not where you *wish* they were.

Why Keyword Research Matters

You might be wondering: *Why can't I just write good content and hope clients find me?* Well, good content is essential, but without the right keywords, even the best content can get lost in the vast ocean of the internet. Keyword research allows you to:

- **Focus on the right audience**: You don't want just anyone visiting your site. You want people who are actively looking for your specific services.
- **Create content that answers real questions**: By using the keywords your clients are searching for, you're directly addressing their concerns, which makes your site more relevant—and more likely to rank well on Google.
- **Get ahead of your competition**: Chances are, other law firms are also trying to rank for similar keywords. Keyword research helps you discover the specific terms

your competitors might be missing, giving you an edge.

How to Find the Right Keywords

Let's dive into the practical side of things: how do you actually find the keywords that your potential clients are searching for? Here's a step-by-step guide to help you uncover the best keywords for your law firm.

Step 1: Brainstorm Keyword Ideas Based on Your Services

Start by thinking about the core services your law firm offers. What kinds of cases do you handle? What are the biggest legal problems your clients face? Once you've listed out your main services, think about how a potential client might search for them.

Example:

Let's say you specialize in personal injury law. Some obvious keyword ideas could be:

- "Car accident lawyer [city]"
- "Slip and fall lawyer near me"
- "How much is a personal injury claim worth?"

If you handle family law, you might start with:

- "Divorce lawyer [city]"
- "How to get custody of my kids"
- "Best family law attorney near me"

The idea is to start with broad, service-based keywords and think about the phrases a potential client would actually type into Google.

Step 2: Use Keyword Research Tools

Once you've brainstormed a few ideas, it's time to take it a step further by using **keyword research tools** to refine and expand your list. These tools will show you how many people are searching for specific terms and give you related keyword suggestions.

Here are a few user-friendly tools you can use to get started:

- **Google Keyword Planner** (Free): Originally designed for Google Ads, this tool is great for discovering keyword ideas and seeing search volumes.
- **Ubersuggest** (Free & Paid): This tool shows keyword suggestions, search volumes, and even your competitors' top-ranking keywords.
- **AnswerThePublic** (Free & Paid): This tool visualizes questions people are asking based on your keyword, helping you get ideas for blog posts and content.

Example:

Let's say you type "car accident lawyer" into Ubersuggest. It might suggest related keywords like:

- "car accident lawyer no win no fee"
- "best car accident lawyer near me"
- "how to hire a car accident attorney"

Each of these variations represents a different way potential clients might search for your services, giving you more options to target in your content.

Step 3: Balance Short-Tail and Long-Tail Keywords

When it comes to keywords, there are two main types to consider: **short-tail** and **long-tail**.

- **Short-tail keywords** are broad, general terms like "divorce lawyer" or "criminal defense attorney." These keywords tend to have high search volumes, but they're also very competitive.

- **Long-tail keywords** are longer, more specific phrases like "best divorce lawyer for men in [city]" or "how much does a DUI lawyer cost." These tend to have lower search volumes, but they're less competitive and often indicate a higher level of intent from the searcher.

Example:

If someone searches for "divorce lawyer," they could be at any stage of their decision process. But if someone searches for "affordable divorce lawyer in [city] with free consultation," they're likely ready to take action. **Long-tail keywords** may have fewer searches, but they often lead to more conversions.

Solution: You need a mix of both short-tail and long-tail keywords. Short-tail keywords help you target broad searches, while long-tail keywords focus on clients who are closer to making a decision.

Step 4: Don't Forget About Local Keywords

As a lawyer, most of your clients are local. That's why **local SEO** is so important, and local keywords are key to your success. Local keywords often include the city, region, or neighborhood where you practice.

Example:

Let's say you're a family law attorney based in Chicago. You wouldn't just optimize your website for "family law attorney." You'd use more specific keywords like:

- "Family law attorney in Chicago"
- "Best divorce lawyer in Chicago"
- "Child custody lawyer near Lincoln Park"

Local keywords help ensure that your website shows up when people in your area are searching for legal help. Google is smart enough to prioritize local results, so including your city or region in your keywords is a must.

Step 5: Analyze Your Competitors' Keywords

Keyword research isn't done in a vacuum. To really succeed, you need to know what your competitors are doing. By analyzing the keywords your competitors are ranking for, you can uncover new opportunities and areas where you can do better.

Here's how to do it:

1. **Search for keywords you want to rank for** in Google, and see which law firms show up on the first page.
2. Use tools like **Ubersuggest** or **SEMrush** to enter your competitors' URLs. These tools will show you what keywords they're ranking for and how much traffic those keywords are driving to their site.

Example:

If a competitor is ranking for "best DUI lawyer in [city]" and you're not, you can create content around that keyword to try and capture some of that traffic. Maybe your competitor isn't targeting long-tail keywords like "affordable DUI lawyer in [city]," which could be an opportunity for you.

How to Integrate Keywords Naturally

Now that you've done your research and found the best keywords, it's time to use them. But here's the thing: you can't just stuff keywords into your website and expect results. Google is smart, and so are your potential clients. Your keywords need to be used **naturally** within your content.

Example of What NOT to Do:

A blog post titled "Best divorce lawyer in [city]" that repeatedly says, "If you're looking for the best divorce lawyer in [city], you've come to the right place. Our best divorce lawyer in [city] is here to help with divorce cases…" is going to sound robotic and spammy.

What TO Do:

Write your content for **humans first**. Use keywords where they make sense, but don't force them. Here's a better example: "Divorce can be a difficult and emotional process. If you're looking for an experienced divorce lawyer in [city], our team is here to help you navigate every step."

Solution:

- Use your primary keyword (e.g., "divorce lawyer in [city]") in the **title tag, meta description**, and **first 100 words** of your content.
- Sprinkle related keywords throughout the content, but make sure it reads naturally.
- Use **synonyms** and related phrases to avoid over-repetition. Google is smart enough to understand context.

Final Thoughts on Keyword Research

Keyword research is the backbone of any successful SEO strategy. By understanding what your potential clients are searching for, you can create content that meets their needs and positions your law firm as the go-to resource. Remember, it's not just about getting more traffic—it's about getting the *right* traffic.

In the next chapter, we'll explore **content creation** and how to turn these keywords into high-quality content that both Google and your clients will love.

CHAPTER 4: CONTENT CREATION FOR LAW FIRMS

Now that you've got your keyword research down, it's time to talk about how to turn those keywords into powerful content. Content is the heart and soul of your website. It's what potential clients will read, and it's how Google will decide whether your site is relevant to the search terms people are using.

In this chapter, we're going to cover how to create content that ranks well on Google and resonates with your audience. But this isn't just about writing any content—it's about crafting **high-quality, keyword-rich content** that helps your law firm stand out from the crowd, build trust with potential clients, and ultimately drive more leads.

The Power of High-Quality, Relevant Content

Let's start with why content is so important. Google loves content. The more valuable and relevant your content is, the more likely Google is to rank your website highly. But Google isn't the only one you're writing for—**you're writing for your potential clients**. The goal of your content is to provide useful, easy-to-understand information that addresses the questions and concerns they have.

When done right, content:

- **Attracts the right visitors**: People searching for legal services are looking for answers. If your content answers their questions, they're more likely to contact you for help.

- **Builds trust**: By providing valuable information, you're positioning yourself as an expert. Potential clients are more likely to choose a lawyer who demonstrates knowledge and authority in their field.

- **Improves SEO**: Google uses content to understand what your site is about and how relevant it is to searchers' queries. The better your content, the higher your chances of ranking.

What Does High-Quality Content Look Like?

High-quality content isn't about writing the longest article or cramming in the most keywords. It's about creating useful, relevant information that solves a problem or answers a question.

Here's what high-quality content should do:

1. **Answer Questions**: Think about what your potential clients are asking Google and make sure your content addresses those questions directly.

2. **Use Plain Language**: Avoid legal jargon. Your clients likely don't understand complex legal terms. Break things down in simple, clear language.

3. **Be Organized and Easy to Read**: Use headings, subheadings, and bullet points to break up your content and make it easy to skim. People rarely read an entire article—they scan for the information they need.

4. **Have a Purpose**: Each piece of content should have a clear goal. Are you trying to educate potential clients? Generate leads? Improve your search rankings? Knowing the purpose will guide how you write.

Types of Content That Work for Law Firms

Not all content is created equal, especially when it comes to SEO. Certain types of content perform better than others. Let's look at a few content types that consistently work well for law firms.

1. Blog Posts: Educate and Engage

Blogs are one of the best ways to create regular, fresh content for your website, which Google loves. They also allow you to target a wide range of keywords and answer common client questions.

Example:

Let's say you're a personal injury attorney. A blog post titled **"What to Do After a Car Accident in [City]"** could target keywords like "car accident lawyer [city]" and "steps after a car accident." In this post, you can walk readers through the immediate steps they should take after an accident while subtly showcasing your expertise.

Best Practices:

- Write about **common questions** clients ask during consultations.
- Use **real-world examples** or hypothetical situations to explain legal processes in a way that clients understand.
- Focus on **local topics** that can attract clients in your area. For example, write about recent changes to the law in your state or city.
- **Keep it conversational**: Blogs don't need to sound like legal documents. Write as though you're explaining things to a friend.

2. Service Pages: Focus on Your Expertise

Your service pages are where you showcase the specific legal services you offer. These pages are crucial because they are often the first place a potential client will land when searching for a lawyer.

Example:

If you're a divorce attorney, your **"Divorce Law Services"** page should focus on explaining what services you offer—like mediation, child custody cases, and alimony disputes. Be sure to weave in local keywords like "divorce lawyer in [city]."

Best Practices:

- Include **primary keywords** in the title and throughout the content, but make sure they flow naturally.
- Clearly explain the **benefits** of working with your firm.
- Use **headings** to break up the content, such as "Our Divorce Services," "Why Choose Us," and "FAQs."
- Include **calls to action** like "Contact us today for a free consultation."

---

3. FAQ Pages: Answer Common Questions

FAQ pages are gold for SEO. They allow you to answer a wide range of client questions in one place, and each question can target a specific long-tail keyword.

Example:

A family law attorney's FAQ page might answer questions like:

- "How long does a divorce take in [state]?"
- "What is the process for getting child custody?"
- "How much does a divorce lawyer cost?"

Best Practices:

- Each question should be a **searchable keyword phrase** that potential clients are typing into Google.
- Keep answers short and to the point. If a question requires a more detailed explanation, link to a blog post or service page with more information.

- Update your FAQs regularly to address new questions or changes in the law.

4. Case Studies: Build Trust Through Success Stories

Potential clients want to know that you've successfully handled cases like theirs before. **Case studies** or **client success stories** help build trust and credibility by showing real examples of how you've helped past clients achieve their legal goals.

Example:

You're a criminal defense attorney, and one of your case studies could describe how you helped a client avoid jail time after being charged with DUI. Use the case study to highlight the challenges, your legal strategy, and the outcome.

Best Practices:

- Keep the focus on **client outcomes** and how your legal expertise made a difference.
- **Protect client confidentiality** by keeping details anonymous.
- Include **quotations** or testimonials from the client if possible.

5. Video Content: Engage with Visual Learners

Video is one of the fastest-growing content types on the web, and it's a powerful tool for law firms. Videos help clients connect with you on a personal level and can break down complicated legal concepts in an engaging way.

Example:

A **"Meet the Attorney"** video on your homepage can introduce yourself, explain your services, and invite clients to reach out for a consultation. You could also create short videos on topics like **"What Happens After a Car Accident?"** or **"How to File for Divorce in [City]."**

Best Practices:

- Keep videos **short and informative** (under 2 minutes is ideal).
- Use **high-quality visuals and sound** to keep the viewer engaged.
- Include a **call to action** at the end of each video, encouraging viewers to contact you or visit your website for more information.

Creating Content for Conversions: Turn Readers Into Clients

It's one thing to get people to your website. It's another to turn those visitors into paying clients. Your content isn't just there to rank on Google—it's also there to convince potential clients that you're the right lawyer for the job.

Here's how to create content that not only attracts visitors but also **converts them into clients:**

1. Include Strong Calls to Action (CTAs)

Every piece of content on your website should have a clear **call to action**. Whether it's "Contact us for a free consultation" or "Call today to discuss your case," you need to guide visitors toward the next step. Make it easy for them to reach out.

Example:

At the end of a blog post about "What to Do After a Car Accident," include a CTA like:

- "If you've been in a car accident, don't wait. Contact our firm today for a free consultation and find out how we can help you get the compensation you deserve."

2. Highlight Your Unique Selling Proposition (USP)

What sets you apart from other law firms? Is it your years of experience? Your personalized approach? Your track record of winning tough cases? Make sure your content highlights your **unique selling proposition (USP)** to show clients why they should choose you over the competition.

Example:

If you specialize in family law, your USP might be:

- **"With over 20 years of experience handling divorce and custody cases in [city], we understand the emotional challenges our clients face and are committed to achieving the best outcomes for families."**

3. Build Trust with Testimonials and Reviews

Client testimonials and online reviews are one of the best ways to build trust with potential clients. When people see that others have had a positive experience with your law firm, they're more likely to reach out to you.

Example:

If you have a testimonial from a past client who was pleased with the outcome of their personal injury case, include it on your website or in a blog post. Something like:

- **"I couldn't be happier with the results from [Your Law Firm]. They handled my case with professionalism and care. I received the compensation I deserved, and they made the process easy to understand. Highly recommend!"**

Final Thoughts on Content Creation

Content is what connects you with potential clients. By creating valuable, relevant, and easy-to-understand content, you're not only improving your chances of ranking well on Google—you're also building trust and showcasing your expertise. When clients feel like you're the authority on their legal issues, they're more likely to pick up the phone and call.

In the next chapter, we'll focus on **local SEO** and how to optimize your law firm's online presence to ensure that clients in your area find you first.

CHAPTER 5: LOCAL SEO – BE THE FIRST FIRM THEY FIND

For most law firms, your clients aren't spread across the country—they're in your city, your neighborhood, or your local region. That's why **local SEO** is so important. When people in your area search for legal services, you want to be the first firm they find.

Local SEO is all about optimizing your online presence to attract clients from your geographic area. Whether they're searching for a "personal injury lawyer near me" or a "family law attorney in [city]," local SEO makes sure you show up at the top of the results, especially in Google's coveted **local pack** (that box of results with a map at the top of the search results page).

In this chapter, we'll cover how to dominate local searches, get listed in the right places, and use reviews to your advantage so that potential clients find your firm first when they need legal help in your area.

What is Local SEO and Why It's Critical for Law Firms?

Local SEO is a strategy that helps your law firm appear in searches when people nearby are looking for legal services. Instead of focusing on broad national keywords, local SEO zeroes in on **location-based keywords**—phrases that include your city, neighborhood, or region. This is especially important for law firms because **legal services are local**. Most clients want a lawyer who is close to them geographically, not someone on the other side of the country.

Here's why local SEO is so crucial:

1. **Clients are searching locally**: When someone needs a lawyer, they typically search for one nearby. If your firm isn't showing up for these local searches, you're missing out on valuable potential clients.

2. **Google prioritizes local results**: Google's algorithm favors local businesses when it detects that a searcher is looking for something nearby. If you're not optimized for local SEO, you won't be part of the top results.

3. **It builds trust**: People trust firms that show up in local search results because they feel more accessible and relevant to their needs. Showing up in local searches also signals to potential clients that you're a trusted expert in your community.

Optimizing for 'Near Me' Searches

When clients search for a lawyer, they often add **"near me"** to their query—things like "car accident lawyer near me" or "divorce lawyer near me." Google knows that these users are looking for local businesses, and it will prioritize firms with strong local SEO.

Example:

Let's say you're a criminal defense lawyer in Chicago. If someone in your area types "criminal defense lawyer near me" into Google, you want your firm to appear in those results. If your local SEO is strong, you'll have a much better chance of showing up at the top of the search.

Here's how to make sure you're optimized for these critical "near me" searches.

Step 1: Claiming and Optimizing Your Google Business Profile

The most important step in local SEO is claiming and optimizing your **Google Business Profile** (formerly Google My Business). Your Google Business Profile is what appears in the **local pack**—that box at the top of search results with a map and a list of local businesses.

Example:

When someone searches for "divorce lawyer in [city]," Google will show a map with the top three local law firms. These businesses aren't necessarily ranked based on their websites alone —Google considers factors like proximity, business information, and reviews. Your Google Business Profile is the key to appearing in this top 3 local pack.

Solution:

- **Claim your Google Business Profile** if you haven't already. You can do this by searching for your business on Google and clicking "Claim this business" or visiting the **Google Business Profile** website to register.
- **Fill out your profile completely**: Make sure you include:
    - **Accurate business information**: Name, address, phone number (known as NAP consistency— more on that below).
    - **Business hours**: Keep them up to date.
    - **Your website link**.
    - **A detailed description of your services**: Include keywords like "family lawyer in [city]" or "criminal defense attorney near [location]."
- **Choose the right categories**: Select specific categories like "Personal Injury Lawyer" or "Family Law Attorney" to help Google understand exactly what you do.
- **Upload high-quality photos**: Pictures of your office, staff, or logo make your listing more engaging.
- **Encourage reviews**: We'll dive deeper into this in a moment, but positive reviews are crucial for local SEO.

Step 2: Building Local Citations and Online Directory Listings

Local citations are mentions of your business name, address, and phone number (NAP) across the web. These mentions can appear in local directories, legal directories, or other relevant websites. The more consistent your NAP is across these listings, the better Google will trust your business—and rank it higher in local searches.

Example:

Let's say your law firm is listed in local directories like **Yelp**, **Avvo**, and **FindLaw**. Google sees these citations as signals that your business is legitimate, and it increases your chances of ranking higher in local searches. If your NAP is inconsistent across directories (for example, your phone number is wrong in one listing), it can confuse Google and hurt your rankings.

Solution:

- Make sure your **Name, Address, and Phone Number (NAP)** is exactly the same across all online listings.
- Get your firm listed in relevant directories, including:
    - **Legal directories**: Avvo, Justia, FindLaw, Martindale-Hubbell.
    - **Local directories**: Yelp, Yellow Pages, your city's Chamber of Commerce website.
    - **Other trusted sites**: Legal blogs, local business directories, and news websites.
- Use tools like **Moz Local** or **Yext** to find inconsistencies in your online listings and correct them.

Step 3: Gathering Local Reviews

When potential clients search for a lawyer, reviews often play a huge role in their decision-making process. Not only do reviews build trust, but they're also a **ranking factor** for local SEO. Google looks at both the quantity and quality of your reviews when deciding where to rank you in local search results.

Example:

Imagine a potential client searching for a family lawyer. They see two firms with similar services, but one has 50 positive reviews, and the other has just 5 mixed reviews. The firm with more positive reviews is likely to attract more clients—and it's also more likely to rank higher in Google's local pack.

Solution:

- **Encourage satisfied clients to leave reviews** on Google. The more positive reviews you have, the better.

- **Respond to all reviews**—both positive and negative. Responding to reviews shows potential clients that you're engaged and care about their feedback.

- **Make it easy for clients to leave reviews**: Send a follow-up email after a successful case with a direct link to your Google Business Profile, asking them to share their experience.

- Avoid **fake reviews** or incentivizing reviews, as this can backfire and damage your credibility.

Step 4: Creating Location-Based Content

To dominate local searches, your website needs to target location-based keywords. One of the best ways to do this is by creating **location-based content**—content that specifically speaks to your geographic area.

Example:

If you're a personal injury lawyer in Houston, a blog post like **"What to Do After a Car Accident in Houston"** can help you rank for searches like "car accident lawyer Houston." Or, if you specialize in family law, you could write a post like **"Filing for**

Divorce in Houston: What You Need to Know." These location-based articles allow you to target local keywords that people in your area are searching for.

Solution:

- **Create local blog posts** that address specific issues in your area. Use headlines that include local keywords like "[Practice Area] Lawyer in [City]" or "How to [Legal Process] in [City]."
- Include **local landmarks or references** in your content. For example, "Our office is located near [landmark], and we've helped clients from all over [city name]."
- Add **location-specific service pages** if your firm serves multiple areas. For example, create a separate page for "Personal Injury Lawyer in [City 1]" and "Personal Injury Lawyer in [City 2]."

Step 5: Optimize for Voice Search

With the rise of smart devices like Alexa and Google Home, **voice search** is becoming increasingly popular, especially for local searches. Voice search queries are often longer and more conversational than text-based searches, and they often include questions like **"Who is the best lawyer near me?"** or **"Find a family law attorney nearby."**

Example:

Someone might use their phone to ask, "Who's the best divorce lawyer near me?" Instead of typing it out, they simply speak the question into their device. These voice searches often focus on local results, so having strong local SEO is crucial for capturing this traffic.

Solution:

- **Optimize your content for conversational, question-based keywords.** For example, instead of just targeting "divorce lawyer [city]," also include phrases like "Who is the best divorce lawyer in [city]?" or "How to find a good divorce attorney near me."

- **Create FAQ sections** on your website that mirror the way people ask questions through voice search. Questions like "How much does a personal injury lawyer cost in [city]?" are great for targeting voice queries.

Step 6: Track and Improve Your Local SEO

Once you've implemented local SEO strategies, it's important to track your progress and make adjustments as needed. Tools like **Google Analytics** and **Google Search Console** can help you monitor which local keywords are driving traffic to your site and how your rankings are improving over time.

Example:

Let's say you notice that your blog post titled "How to Choose a Family Lawyer in [City]" is getting a lot of local traffic. You might decide to write more content around similar topics or further optimize that page to capture even more traffic.

Solution:

- Use **Google Analytics** to track how much local traffic your site is getting and which pages are performing best.
- **Check your rankings** for local keywords using tools like **Moz**, **Ubersuggest**, or **SEMrush** to see if your optimization efforts are paying off.
- **Keep improving your listings** by updating your Google Business Profile, gathering more reviews, and creating fresh, local content.

Final Thoughts on Local SEO

Local SEO is the key to making sure your law firm gets

noticed by the right people—those in your community who are actively looking for legal services. By optimizing your Google Business Profile, gathering reviews, and creating location-specific content, you can dominate local searches and stand out from the competition.

In the next chapter, we'll dive into **link building**, another powerful way to improve your SEO rankings by earning trust from other websites.

CHAPTER 6: LINK BUILDING FOR LAW FIRMS

By now, you've built a strong foundation for your law firm's SEO with a well-optimized website, solid content, and local SEO strategies. But there's one more crucial element that can help take your rankings to the next level: **link building**.

Think of links as votes of confidence from other websites. When another site links to your website, it's essentially telling Google, "This content is valuable and trustworthy." The more high-quality backlinks you have, the better your chances of ranking higher in search engine results. But it's not just about quantity—it's about the **quality** and **relevance** of those links.

In this chapter, we'll cover the basics of link building, why it's so important, and the best strategies for law firms to earn links from reputable websites.

Why Backlinks Matter

Backlinks, also known as **inbound links**, are one of the most important ranking factors in Google's algorithm. When reputable websites link to your site, it signals to Google that your content is authoritative, reliable, and worth ranking higher. But there's more to backlinks than just SEO benefits. Backlinks also help drive **referral traffic**—visitors who click on the link and land on your site from other places on the web.

Here's why backlinks are so important for your law firm:

1. **Improved SEO rankings**: The more high-quality backlinks you have, the more likely Google is to see your site as an authority and rank it higher for relevant searches.
2. **Increased visibility**: Backlinks from reputable sources help you get discovered by new audiences, including people who may not have found your site otherwise.
3. **Builds credibility**: If well-known legal blogs, news outlets, or industry websites are linking to your content, it adds to your firm's credibility in the eyes of both Google and potential clients.

The Difference Between Good and Bad Backlinks

Not all backlinks are created equal. Some backlinks can help you climb to the top of search rankings, while others can drag you down. Google cares about the **quality** of the links pointing to your site, not just the quantity.

Good Backlinks:

- **Come from reputable, relevant websites**: For example, if a legal blog, a news site, or a government website links to your content, Google sees that as a strong vote of confidence.
- **Are earned organically**: These links come from websites that choose to link to your content because it's valuable or informative.
- **Have relevant anchor text**: The text that is hyperlinked should be related to the content it's linking to. For example, if you're a criminal defense lawyer, a good backlink would look like "Learn more about criminal defense strategies."

Bad Backlinks:

- **Come from low-quality, spammy websites**: If your site is being linked to by questionable sites with no relevance to the legal industry, it can hurt your rankings.

- **Are bought or manipulated**: If you're purchasing backlinks or participating in shady link schemes (like link exchanges or link farms), Google can penalize your site.

- **Have irrelevant or generic anchor text**: Links with anchor text like "click here" or "best website" don't add much SEO value, especially if the context isn't related to your firm's services.

Pro Tip: Avoid **"black hat"** SEO tactics like buying links or using link farms. These methods might get you short-term results, but they can lead to long-term penalties from Google, which can be hard to recover from.

Effective Strategies for Earning Quality Backlinks

Now that you understand the importance of good backlinks, let's look at some proven strategies to help your law firm earn high-quality links.

1. Guest Posting on Legal Blogs and Industry Sites

One of the most effective ways to build backlinks is by writing **guest posts** for legal blogs, industry websites, or local news outlets. When you provide valuable, well-written content, most websites will include a link back to your site in the author bio or within the article itself.

Example:

You're a family law attorney and you write a guest post for a popular legal blog about **"The Impact of Divorce on Child Custody in [State]"**. In the author bio, there's a link to your law firm's website. Not only do you get a high-quality backlink, but you also position yourself as an expert in your field.

How to Get Started:

- **Research legal blogs and industry sites** that accept guest posts. Look for sites with high domain authority and relevance to your practice area.
- Reach out to the site's editor with a **well-crafted pitch** offering a guest post. Make sure the topic is relevant to their audience and showcases your expertise.
- **Write high-quality content** that provides value to the site's readers. The better the content, the more likely the site will accept your post and link back to your site.

2. Get Listed in Legal Directories

High-authority legal directories like **Avvo**, **Justia**, and **FindLaw** offer great opportunities for earning backlinks. These directories often have high domain authority, which can boost your SEO while also helping potential clients find you.

Example:

When you create a profile on Avvo, your law firm gets a **backlink** from a trusted legal directory. This not only helps with SEO but also builds credibility when potential clients search for a lawyer in your area.

How to Get Started:

- **Create profiles** on top legal directories like Avvo, Justia, FindLaw, and Martindale-Hubbell.
- **Make sure your profiles are complete** with detailed information about your practice areas, contact information, and your website link.
- Keep your profiles **up to date** and encourage clients to leave reviews on these platforms.

3. Local News and Media Coverage

Getting featured in local news or media outlets can provide you with valuable backlinks while also boosting your firm's visibility. News websites typically have high domain authority, so a link from a news story can do wonders for your SEO.

Example:

Let's say your law firm sponsors a local charity event or provides expert commentary on a legal issue in the news. When the local newspaper covers the event or interviews you, they might include a link to your website.

How to Get Started:

- **Pitch stories** to local news outlets, offering your legal expertise on topics that are relevant to their audience.
- Look for opportunities to **sponsor local events**, which can often lead to media coverage and backlinks.
- Offer to **write op-eds** or provide expert commentary on legal topics for your local paper or online news outlet.

4. Write High-Quality, Linkable Content

One of the best ways to earn backlinks is by creating **high-quality content** that other websites naturally want to link to. This could be blog posts, guides, or resources that offer valuable information for your audience.

Example:

Let's say you write a comprehensive guide on **"How to File for Divorce in [State]"**. This type of evergreen, informative content is something that other websites, blogs, or even local news outlets might link to when discussing divorce laws or resources in your state.

How to Get Started:

- Focus on creating **evergreen content** that will remain

relevant over time.

- Create **data-driven posts, infographics, or legal guides** that are valuable to your audience. These types of resources are more likely to get shared and linked to by others.

- Make sure your content is **well-organized** and easy to read, as this increases the chances of other sites linking to it.

5. Build Relationships with Other Local Businesses

Another great way to build backlinks is by forming partnerships with other **local businesses**. For example, you might collaborate with other professionals who serve the same audience, such as real estate agents, financial advisors, or therapists.

Example:

As a family law attorney, you could build a relationship with a local marriage counselor or financial planner. They might link to your website from their resource pages or blog posts, and in return, you could link to their services from your site.

How to Get Started:

- **Network with other local businesses** and professionals in your area.

- Offer to **exchange guest posts** or contribute to each other's blogs, with backlinks to your respective websites.

- Look for **local events or collaborations** where you can work together and build links naturally.

6. Use HARO (Help a Reporter Out)

Help a Reporter Out (HARO) is a service that connects journalists looking for expert sources with professionals who can provide insights. By signing up for HARO, you can respond to requests from reporters looking for legal expertise. If they use your input, they'll often include a link to your law firm's website in the article.

Example:

A reporter writing a story about personal injury cases might put out a request on HARO for expert commentary. You provide a detailed response, and the article includes a quote from you along with a link to your law firm's website.

How to Get Started:

- **Sign up for HARO** and set up alerts for legal-related topics.
- Respond to relevant requests with **clear, concise, and helpful insights**. The more value you provide, the more likely the reporter will include you in the article.
- Keep an eye out for **opportunities to showcase your expertise** on topics related to your practice areas.

Avoiding Bad Backlinks

While earning backlinks is important, it's just as crucial to avoid **bad backlinks**. Links from low-quality, irrelevant, or spammy websites can hurt your SEO more than help it. If Google sees that your website is associated with questionable sites, it can lower your rankings—or even penalize your site altogether.

How to Avoid Bad Backlinks:

- **Don't buy links**: It might be tempting to pay for backlinks, but this is against Google's guidelines and can lead to penalties.
- **Steer clear of link farms**: These are networks of websites that exist solely for the purpose of linking to each other. They offer no real value and can hurt your SEO.
- **Disavow bad links**: If you discover that your site has links from low-quality or spammy sites, you can use

Google's **Disavow Tool** to tell Google to ignore those links.

Final Thoughts on Link Building

Link building is one of the most powerful tools in your SEO toolkit. By earning high-quality backlinks from reputable sources, you're not only boosting your search rankings but also building trust and credibility with potential clients. Whether through guest posting, local media coverage, or partnerships with other businesses, the right backlinks can drive more traffic and help your firm grow.

In the next chapter, we'll explore **advanced SEO tactics**, including the rise of **voice search**, **video SEO**, and the technical tricks that can give your law firm an edge in the competitive digital landscape.

CHAPTER 7: ADVANCED SEO TACTICS FOR LAWYERS

You've got the basics of SEO down—your website is optimized, your content is top-notch, and you've built a solid foundation of backlinks. Now, it's time to take things to the next level with some **advanced SEO tactics**. These strategies are designed to give your law firm an edge in a competitive landscape by fine-tuning your SEO and capitalizing on the latest trends in search behavior.

In this chapter, we'll dive into technical SEO elements like **schema markup**, **voice search optimization**, and **video SEO**, as well as the importance of continually measuring and improving your SEO performance.

Schema Markup: Helping Google Understand Your Content

Schema markup is a technical SEO tool that helps search engines understand the specific information on your website. It's essentially a type of code that tells Google what your content means, not just what it says. By using schema markup, you can enhance the way your law firm's information appears in search results, making it more visible and attractive to potential clients.

Example:

Imagine you're a criminal defense lawyer, and someone searches for "DUI lawyer in [city]." With the right schema markup, your result could display additional information, such as your law firm's reviews, office hours, and a "Call Now" button, all directly in the search result. This makes your listing stand out and encourages people to click.

Solution:

- Use **legal-specific schema markup** to highlight key details such as practice areas, lawyer profiles, case types, client reviews, and office locations.
- You can also add **FAQ schema** to ensure that your frequently asked questions appear in Google's featured snippets, which is a prime spot on the search results page.

How to Get Started:

- Use Google's **Structured Data Markup Helper** to create schema markup for your website.
- Implement the code on your site or ask your web developer to do it.
- Test your markup using the **Google Rich Results Testing Tool** to ensure it's working correctly.

Optimizing for Voice Search: Capturing Conversational Queries

With the rise of virtual assistants like Alexa, Siri, and Google Assistant, **voice search** has become a huge part of the way people search for information online. Voice searches tend to be longer and more conversational than text searches, and they often focus on local results—making voice search optimization a key component of local SEO for law firms.

Example:

Let's say someone asks, "Who is the best personal injury lawyer near me?" Voice search results typically pull from featured snippets, local business listings, and websites that are optimized for conversational, question-based keywords.

Solution:

- **Optimize for long-tail keywords and natural language queries.** People using voice search often ask full questions, like "How much does a personal injury lawyer cost?" instead of typing just "personal injury lawyer cost."

- Focus on **local optimization**—most voice searches are local, so make sure your law firm's Google Business Profile is up to date and includes your city, practice areas, and relevant keywords.

- **Add an FAQ section** to your website. These are often featured in voice search results, and they naturally match the way people ask questions through voice search.

How to Get Started:

- Use tools like **AnswerThePublic** to find common questions people are asking about your practice area, then incorporate those questions into your website's content.

- Ensure your website is **mobile-friendly**, since most voice searches happen on mobile devices.

- Keep your content **concise and to the point**—Google likes pulling short, clear answers for voice queries.

Video SEO: Boosting Engagement and Rankings

Video content is one of the most engaging and effective forms of content on the web today, and it's only growing in importance. Not only does video help increase time spent on your website (a key ranking factor), but it also gives you an opportunity to rank in **video search results** on both Google and YouTube.

Example:

You create a short explainer video titled **"What to Do After a Car Accident in [City]"** and upload it to YouTube. By optimizing the video's title, description, and tags with relevant keywords, you increase your chances of showing up both in YouTube search results and in Google's video carousel.

Solution:

- **Create short, informative videos** that answer common client questions, explain legal processes, or provide insights into specific practice areas.
- Upload your videos to YouTube and your website, optimizing the **title**, **description**, and **tags** with your target keywords.
- Embed videos on relevant blog posts or service pages to **increase engagement** and time spent on your site.
- Consider adding **transcripts** of your videos to your website, which can improve SEO by giving Google more text to index.

How to Get Started:

- Start by creating videos that answer common questions like **"What happens if I get charged with a DUI?"** or **"How do I file for divorce in [City]?"**
- Use tools like **TubeBuddy** or **VidIQ** to find relevant keywords for your video's title and description.
- Include a **call to action** in each video, encouraging viewers to visit your website or contact your firm for a consultation.

Tracking and Measuring Success: Monitoring Your SEO Performance

To make sure your SEO efforts are working, you need to regularly monitor your website's performance. Tracking your rankings, traffic, and conversions will help you understand what's working, what needs improvement, and where you should focus your future efforts.

Example:

Let's say you notice that a blog post about "What to Do After a Car Accident" is getting a lot of traffic but isn't converting visitors into clients. By reviewing the post's performance in **Google Analytics**, you can identify where visitors are dropping off and optimize the content or add stronger calls to action to increase conversions.

Solution:

- Use **Google Analytics** to track how much traffic your site is getting, where that traffic is coming from, and which pages are performing the best.
- Set up **Google Search Console** to monitor how your site is performing in search results, including which keywords are driving the most traffic.
- Track **conversion rates** to see how well your site is turning visitors into clients. This can include tracking form submissions, phone calls, or clicks on your "Contact Us" button.

How to Get Started:

- Install **Google Analytics** and **Google Search Console** on your website.
- Regularly check your site's performance to identify which pages are bringing in traffic and which need improvement.
- Use **heatmaps** (via tools like Hotjar or Crazy Egg) to see where visitors are clicking and how they navigate through your site.

Staying Ahead of the Curve: The Future of SEO for Law Firms

SEO is constantly evolving, and it's important to stay ahead of the curve to keep your law firm competitive. Here are a few emerging trends that are shaping the future of SEO:

1. **Artificial Intelligence and Machine Learning**: Google's AI-based algorithms (like RankBrain) are getting better at understanding search intent and delivering more personalized results. Make sure your content is **user-focused**, providing clear, helpful information that answers searchers' questions.

2. **Core Web Vitals**: Google has introduced **Core Web Vitals** as a ranking factor, focusing on website speed, responsiveness, and visual stability. Make sure your website provides a **great user experience** by optimizing for these metrics.

3. **Mobile-First Indexing**: Google now uses the mobile version of your website to determine its ranking, so having a mobile-friendly site is more important than ever.

4. **Visual and Image Search**: With advances in image recognition technology, **visual search** is becoming more common. This is particularly relevant for law firms that use imagery or video on their websites. Make sure your **images are optimized** with alt text and descriptive filenames to capture potential image search traffic.

Final Thoughts on Advanced SEO

By incorporating advanced SEO tactics like schema markup, voice search optimization, and video SEO, you're giving your law firm a competitive edge in today's digital landscape. These strategies will help you capture more traffic, increase your online visibility, and ultimately drive more leads.

Remember, SEO is a continuous process. Stay up to date with the latest trends and regularly track your performance to ensure your efforts are paying off. In the next chapter, we'll cover **how to avoid common SEO pitfalls** and what to do if your site encounters a Google penalty.

CHAPTER 8: COMMON SEO PITFALLS AND HOW TO AVOID THEM

SEO can be a game-changer for your law firm, but like any strategy, it's important to avoid common pitfalls that can derail your efforts. Even experienced marketers make mistakes that hurt their search engine rankings, slow down their website traffic, or lead to penalties from Google. The good news is that these mistakes are avoidable—as long as you know what to look for.

In this chapter, we'll walk through the most common SEO mistakes and how you can steer clear of them to ensure your law firm's website continues to rank well and drive valuable traffic.

1. Keyword Stuffing: Less is More

One of the oldest SEO tricks in the book is **keyword stuffing**—the practice of overloading a webpage with keywords in the hope of ranking higher. Unfortunately, this tactic no longer works, and in fact, it can hurt your site's rankings. Google's algorithm is smart enough to recognize when keywords are being forced unnaturally into content, and it rewards sites that use keywords naturally and provide value to readers.

Example of Keyword Stuffing:

You're trying to rank for "divorce lawyer in Chicago," so you write something like this:
"If you're looking for the best divorce lawyer in Chicago, our

divorce lawyer in Chicago can help you with divorce cases in Chicago. Contact our Chicago divorce lawyer today."

This reads terribly for humans and offers no real value to potential clients. It's also likely to get flagged by Google.

Solution:

- Use your **keywords naturally** within your content. If you find that you're repeating the same keyword too many times, consider using variations or synonyms.
- Focus on **writing for humans first, search engines second**. Your goal should be to provide helpful, informative content that answers the questions your clients are asking.
- Use **LSI (Latent Semantic Indexing) keywords**—related terms and phrases that help Google understand your content without needing to repeat the exact same keyword.

2. Ignoring Mobile Optimization: Think Mobile-First

More than half of all web traffic now comes from mobile devices, and Google uses a **mobile-first indexing** system. This means Google primarily uses the mobile version of your website to determine rankings. If your website isn't optimized for mobile, you risk losing not only traffic but also potential clients who find your site difficult to navigate on their smartphones.

Example:

Let's say a potential client searches for "criminal defense lawyer near me" on their phone. They click on your website, but the text is too small, the navigation is clunky, and the site loads slowly. Frustrated, they hit the back button and click on your competitor's site instead.

Solution:

- Make sure your website has a **responsive design** that automatically adjusts to different screen sizes.
- Use Google's **Mobile-Friendly Test** to see how well your site performs on mobile devices.
- Focus on improving **mobile page speed**, **button sizes**, and **font readability** to create a smooth user experience on smaller screens.

3. Not Fixing Broken Links: Keep Your Site Clean

Broken links—links that lead to non-existent pages—hurt your user experience and send negative signals to Google. When visitors click on a link and are met with a "404 error," they're likely to leave your site, which increases your **bounce rate** (a measure of how quickly visitors leave your site). Google interprets high bounce rates as a sign that your site isn't providing a good user experience, which can lower your rankings.

Example:

You've written a blog post about filing for bankruptcy, and you include a link to a government resource. However, over time, the link breaks and now leads to a 404 error page. Visitors who click on it get frustrated, and Google sees it as a poor user experience.

Solution:

- Use tools like **Google Search Console** or **Screaming Frog** to regularly check for broken links on your website.
- **Fix or remove broken links** as soon as possible. Either replace them with updated links or redirect them to relevant, working pages on your site.
- Set up **301 redirects** for pages you've moved or deleted to guide both users and search engines to the correct location.

4. Using Thin or Duplicate Content: Quality Over Quantity

In the past, some websites would churn out low-quality, short articles just to create more pages for search engines to index. This tactic doesn't work anymore. Google now penalizes sites with **thin content**—content that provides little to no value to readers—or **duplicate content**, which appears on multiple pages either within your site or on other websites.

Example:

You create a page for "DUI lawyer services" and then copy the same content across multiple locations on your site with slight modifications for "traffic violation lawyer services" and "criminal defense lawyer services." Not only is this duplicate content, but it doesn't provide unique value for each practice area.

Solution:

- Create **unique, in-depth content** for each page of your website. Every piece of content should serve a purpose and provide real value to your potential clients.
- Avoid duplicating content from other sites or repeating the same information across your own pages. If you need to cover similar topics, take a fresh approach or add additional insights.
- Use **canonical tags** if you have similar content that needs to exist on multiple pages. This tells Google which version of the page is the original.

5. Overlooking Metadata: Missing Out on SEO Basics

Metadata, including **title tags** and **meta descriptions**, is an essential part of SEO that often gets overlooked. These are the snippets of text that appear in search results and help search engines understand what your page is about. Without optimized metadata, you're missing an opportunity to increase your click-through rate (CTR) and improve your rankings.

Example:

You create a service page for "personal injury lawyer services," but your title tag is generic: "Home Page" or "Our Services." This doesn't tell Google or potential clients anything about the content of the page.

Solution:

- Write **descriptive, keyword-rich title tags** for each page of your website. For example, instead of "Home Page," use **"Top Personal Injury Lawyer in [City] – Get a Free Consultation"**.

- Craft **compelling meta descriptions** that summarize the page content and include a call to action, such as **"Injured in an accident? Contact our experienced personal injury attorneys for a free case evaluation."**

- Keep your title tags under 60 characters and meta descriptions under 160 characters to ensure they don't get cut off in search results.

6. Forgetting About Site Speed: Fast is Best

Page speed plays a critical role in both user experience and SEO rankings. Slow-loading websites frustrate visitors and can cause them to leave before the page fully loads. Google considers **page speed** as a ranking factor, so a slow website can significantly hurt your SEO.

Example:

A potential client visits your website to learn about your family law services, but the page takes several seconds to load. Impatient, they click back and choose another firm with a faster-loading site.

Solution:

- Use tools like **Google PageSpeed Insights** or **GTMetrix** to test your site's speed.

- Optimize your website by:
    - **Compressing large images** without sacrificing quality.
    - Reducing the number of unnecessary **plugins** or scripts.
    - Leveraging **browser caching** and **content delivery networks (CDNs)** to speed up load times.
- Aim for a load time of under **3 seconds** to keep users engaged and improve your SEO rankings.

7. Neglecting to Optimize for Local SEO

If your law firm serves clients in a specific geographic area, ignoring **local SEO** can be a costly mistake. Without local optimization, your firm might not show up in search results for "near me" queries or in the **local pack** (the top 3 local results with a map). This means missing out on potential clients right in your community.

Example:

You're a personal injury lawyer in Denver, but when someone searches for "personal injury lawyer near me," your firm doesn't appear in the local results because you haven't optimized your Google Business Profile or used location-based keywords.

Solution:

- **Claim and optimize your Google Business Profile** with accurate information, including your name, address, phone number, business hours, and services.
- Include **location-specific keywords** in your content, such as "divorce lawyer in [City]" or "DUI lawyer near [Neighborhood]."
- Get **positive reviews** from satisfied clients, which help boost your rankings in local search results.

8. Ignoring Google's Algorithm Updates

Google's search algorithm is constantly evolving. Every few months, Google rolls out updates that can impact how websites are ranked. If you're not staying up to date with these changes, you might find your website's traffic or rankings suddenly drop.

Example:

Your site has been ranking well for months, but after a new Google update, you notice a significant drop in traffic. You haven't made any changes to your site, but Google's new algorithm now favors faster, more mobile-friendly websites, and yours isn't up to par.

Solution:

- **Stay informed** about Google's algorithm updates by following industry blogs, Google Search Central, and SEO news sources.
- Regularly **audit your website** to ensure it meets Google's latest standards, especially around **site speed**, **mobile-friendliness**, and **content quality**.
- If you notice a drop in traffic after an update, use **Google Search Console** to identify issues and make the necessary adjustments.

9. Not Tracking SEO Metrics: Measure What Matters

SEO isn't a one-time task—it's an ongoing process that requires regular monitoring and adjustments. If you're not tracking your SEO performance, you won't know what's working, what needs improvement, or how to adapt to changes in search algorithms.

Example:

You've been working on improving your site's SEO for months, but you're not seeing the results you expected. You haven't been tracking which keywords are driving traffic, which pages are performing well, or how visitors are interacting with your site.

Solution:

- Set up **Google Analytics** and **Google Search Console** to track important SEO metrics like organic traffic, keyword rankings, bounce rate, and conversion rates.
- Regularly review your website's performance to identify which pages are driving the most traffic and which keywords are performing well.
- Adjust your SEO strategy based on the data. If a particular blog post is driving a lot of traffic, consider creating more content on similar topics.

Final Thoughts on Avoiding SEO Pitfalls

SEO can be a powerful tool for growing your law firm, but it's important to avoid the common mistakes that can hurt your rankings and drive potential clients away. By focusing on quality content, mobile optimization, local SEO, and regular performance tracking, you'll be well on your way to building a successful SEO strategy that brings in more traffic and leads.

In the next chapter, we'll cover **how to maintain and improve your rankings over time**, ensuring that your law firm continues to thrive in an ever-changing digital landscape.

CHAPTER 9: TRACKING, MEASURING, AND IMPROVING SEO PERFORMANCE

You've built a strong foundation for your law firm's SEO, but as with any marketing strategy, the work doesn't stop once the initial setup is done. SEO is an ongoing process, and to stay ahead of the competition, you need to continuously track, measure, and improve your SEO performance.

In this chapter, we'll cover the key metrics you should be tracking, the tools you can use to measure your progress, and how to adjust your strategy based on data insights. By regularly monitoring your SEO performance, you can identify what's working, fix what's not, and ensure your efforts are driving real results—more traffic, leads, and clients.

The Most Important SEO Metrics to Track

Tracking SEO metrics is like having a roadmap—you can't improve what you don't measure. But with so much data available, it's easy to get overwhelmed. Instead of trying to track everything, focus on the key metrics that will give you actionable insights into your website's performance.

Here are the most important SEO metrics to keep an eye on:

1. Organic Traffic

Organic traffic refers to the visitors who come to your website through unpaid search results. This is one of the most direct indicators of how well your SEO efforts are working. If your organic traffic is increasing, it means more people are finding your website through search engines.

Example:

Let's say you've been optimizing your website for the keyword "personal injury lawyer in [City]." By tracking your organic traffic, you can see if more people are landing on your site after searching for that term.

How to Track:

- Use **Google Analytics** to monitor your organic traffic. Navigate to the "Acquisition" tab, then "All Traffic," and click "Organic Search" to see how many visitors are coming from search engines.
- Check for **trends over time**. Are there spikes or drops in traffic? Are certain pages or keywords driving more traffic than others?

2. Keyword Rankings

Your **keyword rankings** show where your website is appearing in search engine results for specific keywords. Higher rankings mean your site is more visible to potential clients searching for legal services.

Example:

You've optimized your content for "divorce lawyer in [City]," and you want to know if your efforts are paying off. By tracking keyword rankings, you can see if your site is climbing toward the top of the search results.

How to Track:

- Use tools like **Google Search Console, SEMrush,** or **Ubersuggest** to monitor your keyword rankings. These tools show where your site ranks for specific keywords and how those rankings change over time.

- Focus on **your primary keywords** (e.g., "DUI lawyer in [City]") and keep an eye on related long-tail keywords (e.g., "affordable DUI lawyer near me").

3. Click-Through Rate (CTR)

Click-through rate (CTR) is the percentage of people who see your site in search results and actually click on it. A low CTR means that while your site is appearing in search results, it's not convincing enough for people to click through to your website.

Example:

You're ranking on the first page of Google for "criminal defense lawyer near me," but your CTR is lower than expected. This could indicate that your title tags or meta descriptions aren't compelling enough to attract clicks.

How to Track:

- Google Search Console provides data on your **CTR for each keyword**. Go to the "Performance" tab to see how often people click on your site when it appears in search results.

- Improve your CTR by crafting **engaging title tags and meta descriptions** that clearly explain what your page offers and why people should click.

4. Bounce Rate

Your **bounce rate** is the percentage of visitors who land on your site and leave without interacting with any other pages. A high bounce rate can indicate that visitors aren't finding what they're looking for or that your website isn't providing a good user experience.

Example:

You notice that your blog post on "What to Do After a Car Accident" is attracting a lot of traffic, but the bounce rate is over 70%. This could mean that visitors aren't finding the information they need or that your content isn't engaging enough to keep them on the page.

How to Track:

- Use **Google Analytics** to monitor bounce rates for each page on your site. Go to the "Behavior" section and click "Site Content" to see bounce rates across different pages.
- If a page has a high bounce rate, review the content to ensure it's **relevant, engaging, and meets the expectations of your visitors.**

5. Conversion Rate

Ultimately, the goal of your SEO strategy is not just to drive traffic but to **convert visitors into clients**. Your **conversion rate** is the percentage of visitors who take a desired action, such as filling out a contact form, calling your office, or booking a consultation.

Example:

You've been working on SEO for your "personal injury lawyer" page, and you're seeing an increase in traffic. However, your conversion rate hasn't improved. This may indicate that while people are finding your site, they're not convinced to take the next step.

How to Track:

- Set up **conversion tracking** in Google Analytics. This could include tracking form submissions, phone calls, or clicks on your "Contact Us" button.
- Regularly review your conversion data to see which

pages and keywords are driving the most conversions, and adjust your strategy accordingly.

6. Page Speed

As we mentioned earlier, **page speed** plays a crucial role in both user experience and SEO. Slow-loading pages can lead to higher bounce rates and lower rankings, so it's important to monitor your website's speed and make improvements where necessary.

Example:

You notice that your "family law services" page has a higher bounce rate than other pages, and after checking the speed, you find it takes 5 seconds to load. Improving the load time could reduce the bounce rate and keep visitors on your site longer.

How to Track:

- Use **Google PageSpeed Insights** or **GTMetrix** to regularly test your site's load times. These tools will give you specific recommendations for speeding up your site.
- Focus on **compressing images**, reducing **unnecessary scripts**, and using a **content delivery network (CDN)** to improve your site's performance.

Tools for Tracking SEO Performance

There are plenty of tools available to help you track and measure your SEO performance. Here are some of the most useful ones:

1. Google Analytics

Google Analytics is a free tool that provides in-depth insights into how visitors are interacting with your website. It tracks everything from traffic sources to bounce rates to conversion goals.

Key Features:

- Track **organic traffic** to see how many visitors are coming from search engines.
- Monitor **user behavior** to understand which pages are performing well and which need improvement.
- Set up **conversion goals** to track leads and phone calls.

2. Google Search Console

Google Search Console is a free tool that helps you monitor how your website performs in Google search results. It's essential for tracking keyword rankings, indexing issues, and more.

Key Features:

- Monitor your **keyword rankings** and see how they change over time.
- Identify **indexing issues** that might prevent your site from appearing in search results.
- Track **click-through rates** (CTR) and impressions for each keyword.

3. SEMrush

SEMrush is a paid tool that offers a full suite of SEO features, including keyword tracking, competitor analysis, and site audits. It's particularly useful for law firms looking to improve their SEO strategy.

Key Features:

- Track **keyword rankings** and get insights into how your competitors are performing.
- Conduct **site audits** to identify technical SEO issues.
- Use the **Backlink Analysis** tool to see where your backlinks are coming from and find new link-building opportunities.

4. Ubersuggest

Ubersuggest is a budget-friendly SEO tool that provides keyword research, site audits, and backlink data. It's a great option for law firms that want to monitor their SEO without breaking the bank.

Key Features:

- Track your **keyword rankings** and get suggestions for new keywords to target.
- Analyze **competitor websites** to see what's working for them.
- Conduct a **site audit** to find and fix SEO issues.

Regularly Reviewing Your SEO Performance

Tracking SEO metrics is only the first step. To get the most out of your SEO efforts, you need to regularly review your performance, analyze the data, and make adjustments based on what you find.

Here's how to set up a regular SEO review process:

1. **Set Monthly or Quarterly Reviews**: Choose a frequency that makes sense for your law firm, whether it's monthly, quarterly, or bi-monthly.
2. **Review Key Metrics**: During each review, focus on the key metrics we discussed—organic traffic, keyword rankings, conversion rates, and bounce rates.
3. **Identify Areas for Improvement**: Are certain pages performing well while others are underperforming? Are there opportunities to optimize content for better rankings or conversions?
4. **Adjust Your Strategy**: Based on your findings, make changes to your SEO strategy. This might involve updating underperforming content, targeting new keywords, or improving page speed.
5. **Test and Measure**: Implement changes and track their

impact over the next few months to see if your adjustments are improving your SEO performance.

Continuous Improvement: How to Stay Ahead

SEO isn't something you "set and forget." Search algorithms evolve, competitors improve, and user behavior changes. The best law firm websites are those that stay agile, constantly looking for ways to improve and adapt.

- **Create Fresh Content**: Regularly adding new content helps keep your site relevant and gives search engines more opportunities to rank your pages.

- **Optimize Old Content**: Don't just focus on new pages. Review your older content and update it with new keywords, refreshed information, or better formatting.

- **Stay Up to Date on SEO Trends**: SEO best practices are constantly evolving. Make sure you stay informed about Google's algorithm updates and new strategies that could give your site an edge.

Final Thoughts on Tracking and Improving SEO

Tracking and measuring your SEO performance is crucial for maintaining and improving your website's visibility. By focusing on the right metrics—like organic traffic, keyword rankings, and conversion rates—you'll have the insights you need to make data-driven decisions that boost your rankings and drive more clients to your law firm.

In the final chapter, we'll cover how to develop a **long-term SEO strategy** that keeps your firm ahead of the competiti

CHAPTER 10: LONG-TERM SEO STRATEGY – STAY AHEAD OF THE GAME

SEO is not a one-time task, nor is it something that has a clear "finish line." It's a continuous process of monitoring, adjusting, and improving your efforts to stay competitive in a constantly evolving digital landscape. By now, you've set up your law firm's SEO strategy, built high-quality content, and optimized for local search. But how do you ensure long-term success?

In this final chapter, we'll cover how to develop a long-term SEO strategy that will keep your law firm at the top of search results, no matter how the landscape changes. We'll also explore how to future-proof your SEO efforts by staying ahead of trends, maintaining consistent results, and adapting to Google's evolving algorithms.

SEO is a Marathon, Not a Sprint

One of the most important things to understand about SEO is that it takes time to see results. While there may be occasional quick wins, most SEO gains come from consistent, long-term effort. It can take months before you see significant improvements in rankings, traffic, and conversions—but once those improvements happen, they tend to be sustainable.

Example:

You've been steadily optimizing your law firm's website for six months, producing high-quality content and building backlinks. At first, the results are slow, but as you continue to publish useful content and improve your site's user experience, your rankings start to rise. Eventually, your firm's website starts to appear in the top three results for key search terms like "personal injury lawyer in [City]."

Key Takeaway: Patience is essential in SEO. The more effort you put into maintaining your strategy over time, the more likely you are to see sustained, long-term growth in your traffic and rankings.

How to Maintain Your Rankings Over Time

After working hard to get your law firm to the top of Google search results, the last thing you want is to lose your ranking. SEO is highly competitive, and your competitors are always working to overtake your position. Here's how you can maintain your hard-earned rankings over time.

1. Regularly Update Your Content

SEO is not static. Your content needs to stay relevant and up to date to maintain strong rankings. Google values **fresh, accurate content**, so make a habit of revisiting your old blog posts, service pages, and other content to ensure it's still current.

Example:

Let's say you wrote a blog post two years ago about "Changes in Personal Injury Laws in [State]." Laws and regulations may have changed since then, so updating the content with the latest information keeps it accurate and improves your chances of ranking well in the future.

How to Do It:

- Regularly review your **existing content** and update any

outdated information, statistics, or legal changes.
- Refresh your posts with new **examples**, **case studies**, or **client stories** to keep the content engaging.
- Add **internal links** to newer, related content to help Google re-crawl and reindex your updated pages.

2. Build and Maintain Backlinks

Backlinks are a crucial factor in maintaining strong SEO rankings, but they require ongoing effort. Even after you've earned some high-quality backlinks, you'll need to continually build new ones to stay competitive. Additionally, if your existing backlinks are removed or become irrelevant (due to site changes or broken links), it can negatively impact your rankings.

Example:

You've earned a backlink from a well-known legal blog, but the blog has since removed the post that linked to your site. As a result, your backlink profile weakens, and you see a slight dip in rankings for that keyword.

How to Do It:

- Regularly monitor your **backlink profile** using tools like **Ahrefs**, **SEMrush**, or **Moz** to identify lost or broken backlinks.
- Continue reaching out to **industry sites** for guest posts, sponsorship opportunities, or collaboration that can lead to new backlinks.
- Use **internal linking** strategically on your own site to pass authority between pages and improve rankings.

3. Keep an Eye on Competitors

SEO is a competitive space, especially for law firms. Your competitors are likely working on their SEO just as hard as you are, and they may be implementing new strategies that could affect your rankings. Keeping an eye on what they're doing can help you stay one step ahead.

Example:

A competing law firm starts ranking higher than you for "divorce lawyer in [City]," thanks to their recent content strategy. By analyzing their keywords, content, and backlinks, you can adjust your strategy to reclaim your ranking.

How to Do It:

- Use tools like **SEMrush** or **Ahrefs** to track **competitor keywords**, backlinks, and content strategies.

- Review your competitors' **most successful content** and identify areas where you can improve or expand upon their efforts.

- Regularly check the **search results** for your target keywords to see how your site compares to your competitors.

4. Adapt to Google Algorithm Changes

Google updates its algorithm frequently, and these changes can have a significant impact on your rankings. Some updates are minor, while others (like the **Core Web Vitals update** or **Mobile-First Indexing**) can cause major shifts in the way websites are ranked. Staying informed about these updates and adapting your strategy accordingly is critical to long-term SEO success.

Example:

Google rolls out an update that prioritizes page speed and user experience. Your site's rankings drop because your pages are slow to load. By improving your site's performance and meeting the new standards, you can regain your rankings.

How to Do It:

- Stay up to date on Google's algorithm changes by following SEO news sources like **Search Engine Journal** and **Moz Blog**.
- Regularly perform **site audits** using tools like **Google Search Console** or **SEMrush** to ensure your site is meeting Google's current ranking criteria.
- If your rankings drop after an update, identify the specific factors that may have caused the issue and make improvements quickly.

SEO Trends to Watch

SEO is constantly evolving, and staying ahead of the latest trends is essential for long-term success. Here are a few SEO trends that are shaping the future of search engine optimization:

1. Voice Search Optimization

As smart speakers and voice-activated search assistants like **Siri** and **Alexa** become more popular, **voice search** is changing the way people find information online. Voice searches tend to be longer and more conversational than traditional text searches, and they often prioritize local results.

How to Stay Ahead:
- Optimize your content for **question-based keywords**. Focus on natural, conversational language in your blog posts and FAQ pages.
- Use **long-tail keywords** that match the way people speak when asking questions out loud (e.g., "What's the best personal injury lawyer near me?").

2. Core Web Vitals and User Experience

Google's focus on **Core Web Vitals**—which measure page load time, interactivity, and visual stability—signals that **user**

experience is becoming a major ranking factor. A site that loads quickly, is easy to navigate, and doesn't shift around as users scroll will have a better chance of ranking well.

How to Stay Ahead:

- Continuously monitor your **site speed** and **mobile responsiveness** using **Google PageSpeed Insights** and other tools.
- Make sure your site delivers a seamless user experience across all devices, especially mobile, since Google prioritizes **mobile-first indexing**.

3. Video and Image Search

As visual content becomes more important, **video SEO** and **image search** are areas where law firms can gain an edge. Optimizing videos and images for search can help your firm reach a broader audience and increase engagement.

How to Stay Ahead:

- Regularly produce and optimize **short, informative videos** that address common legal questions or offer advice.
- Use **descriptive alt text** and **file names** for all images and videos on your site to improve your chances of appearing in Google's image and video search results.

Building a Digital-First Law Firm

As more people turn to the internet for legal services, it's crucial for your law firm to embrace a **digital-first mindset**. This means making SEO, content marketing, and online engagement an integral part of your long-term growth strategy. Here's how to build a digital-first law firm that thrives in the modern landscape:

1. Prioritize Your Online Presence

Your website is your digital storefront, and it's often the first impression potential clients will have of your firm. Make sure it's professional, user-friendly, and optimized for search engines.

How to Do It:

- Regularly update your website with **fresh content** that answers potential clients' legal questions and addresses their needs.
- Invest in ongoing **SEO efforts** to ensure your site continues to rank well for relevant search terms.
- Stay active on **social media** and other online platforms to engage with your audience and share valuable content.

---

2. Create a Sustainable Content Marketing Plan

Content marketing should be a core part of your long-term SEO strategy. Regularly producing helpful, informative content that aligns with your target audience's needs will help you attract and retain clients over time.

How to Do It:

- Develop a **content calendar** that outlines your blog posts, videos, and other content for the next six months to a year.
- Focus on creating **evergreen content**—content that remains valuable and relevant long after it's published.
- Use **data and insights** from your SEO tracking tools to guide your content strategy and optimize for performance.

---

3. Continue Building Relationships Online

Networking doesn't only happen at conferences or local events—it happens online, too. Building relationships with industry leaders, legal bloggers, and local businesses can help you expand your digital reach and earn valuable backlinks.

How to Do It:

- Regularly participate in **guest blogging**, webinars, or interviews to increase your online visibility and build your authority.

- Engage with **other professionals** and organizations in your area by sharing their content, collaborating on projects, and referring clients when appropriate.

Final Thoughts: SEO as a Long-Term Investment

SEO is a long-term investment in your law firm's future. The strategies you implement today may not yield immediate results, but over time, they'll help you build a powerful online presence that consistently brings in clients. The key to staying ahead is to remain proactive—tracking your performance, staying informed about industry trends, and adapting to changes in the digital landscape.

By following the strategies outlined in this book, you've laid the groundwork for a successful SEO journey. Now, it's time to take that foundation and build on it for sustained growth and long-term success.

Conclusion: Your SEO Journey Begins Now

You've now completed **Lawyer's SEO Playbook**, and you're armed with the tools and knowledge to optimize your law firm's website, attract more clients, and grow your practice through SEO. Remember, SEO isn't a one-time project—it's an ongoing effort that requires patience, consistency, and a commitment to delivering value to your clients.

Whether you're just starting out or you've been running your law firm for years, SEO is one of the most effective ways to build your brand, stand out from the competition, and ensure your firm continues to thrive in the digital age. Now it's time to put these strategies into action and watch your firm grow.

CONCLUSION: PUTTING IT ALL TOGETHER – YOUR PATH TO SEO SUCCESS

You've made it through the **Lawyer's SEO Playbook**, and by now, you've gained a comprehensive understanding of how to use SEO to grow your law firm's online presence, attract more clients, and stand out in a competitive market. From the foundational elements like keyword research and content creation to advanced strategies like link building and voice search optimization, you're now equipped to take control of your law firm's digital future.

Let's take a moment to recap what you've learned and highlight some final tips to ensure you get the most out of your SEO efforts.

Key Takeaways from the Lawyer's SEO Playbook

1. The Power of SEO for Law Firms

We began by understanding why SEO is critical for law firms in today's digital world. Clients are increasingly turning to Google to find legal services, and SEO ensures that your law firm is visible to the right people at the right time. You've learned how SEO drives organic traffic, builds credibility, and helps you attract the clients who need your services.

Tip: Make sure your website is always optimized with strong

keywords and delivers value to your visitors, as this is the foundation of good SEO.

2. Building a Strong SEO Foundation

In the early chapters, we covered the importance of **technical SEO** and creating a website that's fast, mobile-friendly, and easy for Google to crawl. Without a solid foundation, all the SEO strategies in the world won't be enough to rank well.

Tip: Regularly audit your website for performance issues, broken links, and mobile responsiveness to ensure it's optimized for both users and search engines.

3. Content is King

Content creation became the heart of your SEO strategy. From blog posts and service pages to FAQs and videos, high-quality content not only helps you rank for important keywords but also builds trust with potential clients. Remember, your content should answer real questions and solve problems for your audience.

Tip: Continuously create and update your content to ensure it remains relevant, useful, and aligned with your target clients' needs.

4. Local SEO: Becoming the Go-To Firm in Your Area

For law firms, **local SEO** is essential. You've learned how to optimize for "near me" searches, build out location-based content, and enhance your visibility in the **local pack** by claiming and optimizing your Google Business Profile. Local SEO ensures that your firm shows up when clients in your community are looking for legal help.

Tip: Don't forget to ask satisfied clients to leave positive reviews on your Google Business Profile to boost your local credibility and rankings.

5. Building Authority with Backlinks

We dove deep into the importance of **backlink building** and how earning links from reputable websites helps Google see your firm as a trusted authority. Whether through guest posting, local media coverage, or collaborations with other businesses, backlinks are a powerful ranking signal that help push your site up the search results.

Tip: Focus on earning backlinks naturally by building relationships with industry websites and producing content that others want to link to.

---

6. The Role of Advanced SEO Tactics

In the later chapters, we covered advanced tactics like **schema markup**, **voice search optimization**, and **video SEO**. These strategies help you stay competitive and prepare your law firm for future trends in search behavior. Whether through structured data, conversational keywords for voice search, or engaging videos, these techniques can set you apart from the competition.

Tip: Keep an eye on emerging SEO trends and adopt new technologies early to stay ahead of the curve.

---

7. Tracking and Improving Your SEO Performance

Finally, we emphasized the importance of **tracking your SEO performance**. SEO isn't a one-and-done task—it's an ongoing process that requires regular monitoring and adjustments. By tracking key metrics like organic traffic, keyword rankings, and conversion rates, you can refine your strategy and continue improving your results.

Tip: Set aside time each month to review your SEO metrics and make data-driven decisions to optimize your efforts.

Your SEO Success Formula

SEO may seem overwhelming at first, but it boils down to a simple formula:

- **Create high-quality content** that answers your clients' questions.
- **Optimize your site** technically to make it fast, mobile-friendly, and easy to navigate.
- **Build backlinks** and **local credibility** to increase your authority in your community.
- **Monitor and adapt** your strategy based on data and changing trends.

When you consistently follow this formula, SEO becomes not just a way to improve your rankings but a powerful marketing tool that drives sustainable growth for your law firm.

The Future of SEO and Your Law Firm

As we've discussed throughout the book, SEO is constantly evolving. Search algorithms change, new trends emerge, and client behavior shifts. But one thing remains constant: the value of delivering high-quality, relevant information that helps people solve their legal problems.

By embracing SEO as a long-term investment in your firm's success, you're setting yourself up for continued growth in the digital age. As your firm grows, so too will the importance of maintaining your online presence and adapting to new opportunities.

Final Thoughts: Start Now, Stay Consistent

If there's one final piece of advice I can leave you with, it's this: **Start now, and stay consistent**. SEO rewards those who put in the time and effort to build a strong online presence over the long haul. The sooner you start implementing the strategies we've covered, the sooner you'll see results.

Remember, the competition is fierce, but with the right approach, you can stand out and attract the clients you need to grow your law firm.

Your journey to SEO success starts here. Now it's time to put these strategies into action and watch your law firm thrive.

Good luck—and here's to your future success!

BONUS CHAPTER: SEO CHEAT SHEET FOR LAWYERS

Building a successful SEO strategy for your law firm can feel overwhelming, but with the right tools and a clear roadmap, you can simplify the process. This cheat sheet provides a quick, easy reference to the most important SEO tactics and best practices covered in this book. Keep it handy as you work on optimizing your website and growing your firm's online presence.

1. Keyword Research Cheat Sheet

Goal: Find the keywords your potential clients are searching for.

- **Start with your practice areas**: List out the main services you offer (e.g., personal injury lawyer, estate planning, family law).
- **Use keyword tools**: Google Keyword Planner, Ubersuggest, or SEMrush to find high-traffic, relevant keywords.
- **Balance short-tail and long-tail keywords**:
    - Short-tail: "DUI lawyer"
    - Long-tail: "Best DUI lawyer near me in [City]"
- **Focus on local keywords**: Include location-specific terms like "divorce lawyer in [City]."

2. On-Page SEO Cheat Sheet

Goal: Optimize individual pages to rank higher on search engines.

- **Title Tags**: Use primary keywords in the title, under 60 characters (e.g., "Top Personal Injury Lawyer in [City] | Free Consult").
- **Meta Descriptions**: Include keywords and a call to action, under 160 characters (e.g., "Need a personal injury lawyer in [City]? Contact us for a free consultation").
- **Headings (H1, H2, H3)**: Use keyword-rich headings to structure your content.
- **URL Structure**: Keep URLs short and include keywords (e.g., www.yourlawfirm.com/personal-injury-lawyer).
- **Internal Linking**: Link related pages to each other within your site (e.g., blog posts linking to service pages).
- **Alt Text for Images**: Add descriptive alt text to images, including keywords where appropriate.

3. Technical SEO Cheat Sheet

Goal: Ensure your website is easy to crawl and index by search engines.

- **Mobile-Friendly Design**: Use a responsive design that adapts to all devices.
- **Page Speed**: Aim for under 3 seconds. Compress images, reduce plugins, and use browser caching.
- **Secure Your Site (HTTPS)**: Install an SSL certificate to ensure your site is secure.
- **Fix Broken Links**: Use tools like Google Search Console to check and fix broken links.

- **Create and Submit a Sitemap**: Use Google Search Console to submit your sitemap to ensure all pages are indexed.

4. Local SEO Cheat Sheet

Goal: Rank for local searches and become the go-to law firm in your community.

- **Google Business Profile**:
    - Claim and fully optimize your listing (accurate name, address, phone number, hours).
    - Use keywords in your business description (e.g., "Experienced divorce lawyer in [City]").
    - Upload high-quality photos and videos of your office.
- **Get Reviews**: Encourage satisfied clients to leave Google reviews. Respond to all reviews, both positive and negative.
- **Citations**: Ensure consistent name, address, and phone number (NAP) information across all online directories.
- **Local Keywords**: Use city or region-specific keywords in your content and meta tags (e.g., "family lawyer in [City]").

5. Content Creation Cheat Sheet

Goal: Create high-quality, SEO-optimized content that attracts and converts potential clients.

- **Focus on client questions**: Answer common legal questions or provide advice (e.g., "What to do after a car accident in [City]?").
- **Use long-form content**: Aim for 1,000+ words to cover topics in depth and rank higher in search results.

- **Create various content types**: Blogs, FAQs, case studies, and videos.
- **Use a clear CTA**: Every page or blog should have a call-to-action (e.g., "Contact us for a free consultation").
- **Consistency is key**: Publish new content regularly to keep your website fresh and relevant.

6. Link Building Cheat Sheet

Goal: Earn high-quality backlinks to build authority and improve rankings.

- **Guest Blogging**: Write guest posts for legal or local blogs with a link back to your website.
- **Legal Directories**: List your firm on high-authority legal directories (Avvo, Justia, FindLaw).
- **Local Media**: Reach out to local newspapers or TV stations to offer legal commentary in exchange for a backlink.
- **Content Promotion**: Promote your blog posts on social media and collaborate with other local businesses to increase shares and links.

7. Tracking and Measuring SEO Cheat Sheet

Goal: Regularly monitor your SEO performance and make data-driven improvements.

- **Google Analytics**: Track organic traffic, bounce rates, and conversions.
- **Google Search Console**: Monitor keyword rankings, click-through rates (CTR), and indexing issues.
- **Page Speed Tools**: Use Google PageSpeed Insights to check and optimize load times.

- **Keyword Tools**: Use SEMrush, Ahrefs, or Ubersuggest to track your keyword performance and identify new opportunities.

8. Avoiding Common SEO Mistakes

Goal: Steer clear of common pitfalls that can hurt your rankings.

- **Avoid keyword stuffing**: Use keywords naturally in your content—don't force them.
- **Watch out for thin or duplicate content**: Every page should offer unique, valuable information.
- **Fix broken links**: Regularly audit your site and fix any broken links or outdated pages.
- **Stay mobile-friendly**: Test your site's mobile responsiveness regularly to avoid losing mobile traffic.
- **Keep an eye on Google's algorithm updates**: Adapt your strategy to align with Google's latest changes.

Final SEO Tip

Stay Consistent: SEO is a long-term strategy. Regularly review your website's performance, continue creating valuable content, and adapt to trends to ensure your law firm's growth over time.

Bonus: Complete Roadmap for Optimizing Your Law Firm's SEO

Ready to take your law firm's SEO strategy to the next level? Follow this **10-step roadmap** to guide you through the entire process, from setting the foundation to ongoing optimization. Use this as your checklist for building a strong, optimized digital presence.

Step 1: Perform an SEO Audit of Your Website

Before diving into optimizations, you need to know where you currently stand. An SEO audit will identify any technical issues, content gaps, or areas for improvement.

- Use tools like **Google Search Console**, **Google Analytics**, and **SEMrush** to assess your site's health.
- Identify any **broken links**, slow pages, missing meta tags, or mobile usability issues.
- Create a list of action items based on your findings.

Step 2: Conduct Keyword Research

To rank well in search engines, you need to understand what keywords potential clients are using to find law firms like yours.

- List out your **practice areas** and the legal services you offer.
- Use tools like **Google Keyword Planner**, **Ubersuggest**, or **SEMrush** to identify high-traffic, relevant keywords.
- Prioritize **local keywords** (e.g., "personal injury lawyer in [City]") to target your immediate audience.
- Find a balance between **short-tail** and **long-tail keywords** to capture a wider range of search intents.

Step 3: Optimize Your Website for On-Page SEO

On-page SEO ensures that your individual web pages are optimized for search engines and provide a great user experience.

- Use your target keywords in **title tags**, **meta descriptions**, and **headings**.
- Structure content with **H1, H2, and H3 headings** to make it easy to read and understand.
- Create clear, concise **URLs** that include relevant keywords.
- Add **internal links** between related pages to guide visitors through your site.
- Optimize **images** with alt text and compress them to improve page load times.

Step 4: Focus on Technical SEO

Your website needs to be easy for search engines to crawl and index. Fix any underlying technical issues that could be hurting your rankings.

- Ensure your website is **mobile-friendly** and responsive across all devices.
- **Increase page speed** by compressing images, reducing unnecessary scripts, and enabling browser caching.
- Install an **SSL certificate** to secure your site (HTTPS).
- Submit a **sitemap** to Google Search Console and create a **robots.txt** file to guide search engine crawlers.
- Check for and fix any **broken links** that result in 404 errors.

Step 5: Create SEO-Optimized Content

Content is the foundation of a good SEO strategy. Create useful, valuable, and engaging content that answers potential clients' legal questions.

- Develop **blog posts, guides, FAQs, and case studies** that target your core keywords.

- Focus on creating **long-form content** (1,000+ words) that covers topics in depth and provides real value to readers.
- Include **local references** (city, region, state) in your content to target local clients.
- Make sure every piece of content includes a **clear call to action (CTA)**, like "Contact us for a free consultation."

Step 6: Optimize for Local SEO

Most law firms rely on local clients, so it's crucial to optimize for **local searches** and ensure that your firm shows up in local search results.

- **Claim and optimize your Google Business Profile** by filling out accurate business information (name, address, phone number, hours).
- Encourage clients to leave **Google reviews**, and respond to all reviews.
- Use **location-specific keywords** in your content and meta tags (e.g., "family lawyer in [City]").
- Build **local citations** by listing your law firm in online legal directories (Avvo, Justia, FindLaw) and local directories (Yelp, Chamber of Commerce).

Step 7: Build High-Quality Backlinks

Earning high-quality backlinks from reputable websites signals to Google that your content is valuable and authoritative.

- Write **guest posts** for legal blogs or industry websites and include backlinks to your site.
- Get listed in **high-authority legal directories** (Avvo,

Martindale-Hubbell, Justia).

- Partner with **local businesses** for referrals and backlinks.
- Use **Help a Reporter Out (HARO)** to provide legal expertise for journalists in exchange for backlinks.

Step 8: Monitor Your SEO Performance

Track your SEO progress to see what's working and where improvements can be made. Use the data to refine your strategy and ensure long-term success.

- Set up **Google Analytics** and **Google Search Console** to track key metrics like organic traffic, keyword rankings, and bounce rates.
- Monitor your **keyword performance** using tools like **SEMrush** or **Ahrefs** to see where you're ranking and how those rankings change over time.
- Track your **conversion rates** to measure how well your site is turning visitors into clients.
- Use heatmaps (via **Hotjar** or **Crazy Egg**) to see how users interact with your site.

Step 9: Stay Updated with Google Algorithm Changes

Google frequently updates its algorithm, which can affect how your site ranks. Stay informed on these updates to ensure your strategy adapts to the latest best practices.

- Follow SEO news from sources like **Search Engine Journal**, **Moz Blog**, and **Google Search Central**.
- Regularly audit your website for any issues that could be impacted by algorithm changes (site speed, mobile-friendliness, content quality).

- Adapt your strategy based on any significant shifts in search engine optimization requirements.

Step 10: Keep Improving and Refining Your Strategy

SEO is an ongoing process that requires continuous effort. Regularly review and refine your SEO strategy to keep up with new trends, improve your performance, and maintain your rankings.

- **Update older content** with new information, keywords, and examples to keep it relevant.
- Identify new content opportunities based on **client questions** and **current trends** in your practice areas.
- Stay proactive in **building backlinks** and maintaining a strong online presence.
- Experiment with **advanced SEO tactics** like video SEO, schema markup, and voice search optimization to stay ahead of competitors.

Final Thoughts on Your SEO Roadmap

By following this **10-step roadmap**, you're creating a solid foundation for your law firm's SEO strategy. Remember, SEO is not a one-time effort but a continuous process of refining, optimizing, and adapting to changes in search engine algorithms and user behavior. With patience and consistent work, your law firm will reap the benefits of improved rankings, increased traffic, and a steady stream of new clients.

Now, it's time to put this roadmap into action and start optimizing your law firm's digital presence!

GLOSSARY

Alt Text

A text description added to images on a website, helping search engines understand the image's content and improving accessibility for users with visual impairments.

Anchor Text

The clickable text in a hyperlink that leads to another page or website. Optimized anchor text is relevant to the linked content and includes keywords.

Backlink

A link from one website to another. Backlinks are an important ranking factor in SEO, as they signal to search engines that other websites consider your content valuable.

Bounce Rate

The percentage of visitors who navigate away from a website after viewing only one page. A high bounce rate can indicate that visitors aren't finding what they need on the page or that the page isn't engaging.

Canonical Tag

A piece of HTML code that tells search engines which version of a page is the "main" version when duplicate content exists, helping avoid ranking issues caused by content duplication.

Click-Through Rate (CTR)

The percentage of users who click on a website link after seeing it in search engine results. A higher CTR indicates that the website's title and description are compelling to users.

Conversion Rate

The percentage of website visitors who take a desired action, such as filling out a contact form, booking a consultation, or making a phone call. This is a key metric for measuring the effectiveness of a website.

Core Web Vitals

A set of metrics Google uses to measure user experience based on page loading speed, interactivity, and visual stability. Core Web Vitals are now an important ranking factor for websites.

Crawling

The process by which search engines use bots (also called spiders or crawlers) to scan a website's pages, gathering information about content, links, and structure to index for search results.

Domain Authority (DA)

A score (developed by Moz) that predicts how well a website will rank on search engines. It ranges from 1 to 100, with higher scores indicating greater authority and ranking potential.

Google Business Profile (formerly Google My Business)

A free business listing that appears in local search results and Google Maps. Optimizing this profile helps businesses rank higher in local SEO and show up for "near me" searches.

Indexing

The process by which search engines store and organize the information from websites to be displayed in search results. If a page isn't indexed, it won't appear in search results.

Internal Link

A link from one page on a website to another page on the same website. Internal links help users navigate a site and improve search engine understanding of the site's structure.

Keyword

A word or phrase that users type into a search engine when

looking for information. SEO strategies focus on optimizing content around keywords to rank higher in search results for relevant searches.

Keyword Research

The process of finding and analyzing the terms that potential clients use to search for legal services. Effective keyword research helps guide content creation and SEO strategies.

Latent Semantic Indexing (LSI) Keywords

Related terms and phrases that provide context to a webpage's content. LSI keywords help search engines better understand the content's relevance without relying on the overuse of a single keyword.

Local Pack

A section of Google's search results that highlights the top three local businesses related to the search query, often displayed alongside a map. Appearing in the Local Pack is key to local SEO success.

Long-Tail Keyword

A longer, more specific keyword phrase that typically has lower search volume but higher conversion rates. Long-tail keywords are often easier to rank for and align closely with user intent.

Meta Description

A brief summary of a webpage's content that appears under the title in search engine results. A well-written meta description can improve click-through rates.

Mobile-First Indexing

Google's approach to indexing websites based on their mobile version, not the desktop version. This shift makes mobile-friendliness a critical factor in SEO rankings.

NAP (Name, Address, Phone Number)

A crucial component of local SEO. NAP consistency across a law firm's website and online directories helps ensure better local search rankings.

Off-Page SEO

SEO strategies that occur outside of your website, such as building backlinks, social media engagement, and influencer outreach, which help boost your site's credibility and authority.

On-Page SEO

SEO strategies implemented on your website to improve rankings, such as optimizing content, title tags, meta descriptions, headings, and internal links.

Organic Traffic

Website visitors who come to your site through unpaid (organic) search engine results rather than through paid ads. Organic traffic is a key measure of SEO success.

Page Speed

The time it takes for a webpage to fully load. A faster page speed improves user experience and is a ranking factor in SEO.

Robots.txt

A file that gives search engines instructions on which pages of a website they can or cannot crawl. This helps prevent unnecessary pages from being indexed.

Schema Markup

A form of structured data that helps search engines understand the content on your website. Schema markup can enhance your search result listings by displaying rich snippets, such as star ratings or FAQs.

Search Engine Results Pages (SERPs)

The pages displayed by search engines in response to a user's query. SEO aims to get your website as high as possible in the SERPs for relevant search terms.

Sitemap

A file that lists all the pages of a website, helping search engines discover and index its content more effectively. Submitting a sitemap to Google Search Console improves a site's crawlability.

Title Tag

An HTML tag that defines the title of a webpage and appears in search engine results as the clickable headline. Optimizing title tags with keywords is crucial for SEO.

Voice Search

A search query made through a voice assistant like Siri, Alexa, or Google Assistant. Optimizing for voice search involves using conversational, question-based keywords.

White-Hat SEO

SEO techniques that follow Google's guidelines and best practices, focusing on long-term growth through high-quality content, ethical link building, and user-focused strategies.